The Crucifixion of Hyacinth

The Crucifixion of Hyacinth

Jews, Christians, and Homosexuals from Classical Greece to Late Antiquity

Geoff Puterbaugh

Preface
by
Wayne R. Dynes

Authors Choice Press
San Jose New York Lincoln Shanghai

The Crucifixion of Hyacinth
Jews, Christians, and Homosexuals from Classical Greece to Late Antiquity

All Rights Reserved © 2000 by Geoff Puterbaugh

No part of this book may be reproduced or transmitted in any form or by any means, graphic, electronic, or mechanical, including photocopying, recording, taping, or by any information storage or retrieval system, without the permission in writing from the publisher.

Authors Choice Press
an imprint of iUniverse.com, Inc.

For information address:
iUniverse.com, Inc.
620 North 48th Street, Suite 201
Lincoln, NE 68504-3467
www.iuniverse.com

ISBN: 0-595-13057-7

Printed in the United States of America

This book is dedicated
to those who suffered,
to those who were imprisoned,
and to those who died.

PREFACE

As the twentieth century draws to a close, interest in history seems to be fading. For many only the present and the future count. The dismissal of the past has filtered down to the elementary-school level. We hear children playing street games in which the person "shot" is signed off: "You're history."

Yet for those of us struggling to discard the mantle of stigma and marginalization that has been cast upon us, history is very real: we live with its consequences. The era that saw the transition from antiquity to the Middle Ages is of pivotal significance. While Græco-Roman society may not have been, as some have nostalgically claimed, a sexual paradise, it stands in stark contrast to the historical stage that followed. For this reason, there can never be enough analysis of this fateful era of transition.

Geoff Puterbaugh's book offers a series of revealing glimpses, allowing the reader to meditate on the continuing significance of various aspects. Commendably, he avoids the technical language in which specialists are wont to envelope this vital subject, vigorously stating the facts and his views. Each chapter includes a series of reference notes so that the interested reader can pursue the matter further.

This book is notably enlivened with quotations from original literature of the periods discussed. While the quotations from scriptural and legal admonitions are essential for the documentation of repression and its rationale, the gay-positive poetry offers a refreshing—and necessary—balance, showing the feelings and experiences of people who were, so it seems, less encumbered with taboos and hesitations than we ourselves—even though we are shuffling off the old prejudices.

Geoff Puterbaugh's book invites the reader to think fruitfully about the relation of the past and the present. Everyone who has read it will emerge with a better understanding of the crucial centuries in which the Western sex ethic, for better or worse, was forged.

Professor Wayne R. Dynes
Hunter College,
City University of New York

Acknowledgments

The author extends special thanks to John Lauritsen, Warren Johansson, and Wayne R. Dynes, who asked important questions and stimulated my initial research. Several men generously offered their time in finding and correcting errors of fact and interpretation: Giovanni Dall'Orto, Wayne R. Dynes, David F. Greenberg, Stephen Wayne Foster, Stephen O. Murray and Norman Larson have my deep gratitude.

Any remaining errors are, of course, my own responsibility.

Contents

Preface vii
Acknowledgments ix
Foreword xiii

Paideia and Pederasty 1
Socrates and Plato...8
Aristotle 19
Greece: the Evidence of Literature 26
Greece: the Legal Position..39
The World of Rome 41
Rome: the Evidence of Literature 46
Rome: the Legal Position 48
The Mosaic Tradition 54
The Kedeshim 64
The Messianic Tradition 68
Jew and Greek in Conflict 75
The World of Hellenism..78
Philo of Alexandria 88
Jesus 99
St. Paul...106
Animal Allegories 113
Clement of Alexandria 117
The Triumph of Fanaticism 130

The Conversion of Constantine 134
The Establishment of Christianity 143
The Death of Zeus 149
The Fall of Rome 151

Afterword 155
Appendix A:
St. John Chrysostom's Defense of Monasticism..............................159
Appendix B:
Edward Gibbon's Sexual Intolerance 167
Bibliography 171
Index 175

Foreword

Much has been written on the history of Europe during the period of transition between paganism and Christianity.

The years that saw the establishment of Christianity as the state religion of the late Roman Empire (324 A.D., under the emperor Constantine) also saw an extraordinary rise in religious and sexual intolerance. The rise of intolerance can be clearly seen in Edward Gibbon's chronicle, *The Decline and Fall of the Roman Empire*, which remains a standard work on the era, and one of the greatest histories written in English. Since Gibbon's work was done during the Enlightenment, and appeared in the late eighteenth century, it needs to be supplemented with the contributions of later historians; his work did not end all research into late antiquity, and the period remains a constantly fascinating specialty of historical research.

To describe this transition between paganism and Christianity, it is necessary to survey a number of large historical and cultural entities, entities which we conveniently give labels such as "Ancient Greece" or "paganism" or "the Roman Empire." None of these things becomes a monolithic whole simply by receiving a label. "Paganism" was not a simple and unified set of beliefs, but rather a complex set of assumptions which varied with time and place. "Ancient Greece" includes both Sparta and Athens (very different places), as well as Boetia, Corinth, and many other entities with a wide dispersion in time and place. "The Roman Empire" was a constantly changing form of government, and its collapse did not lead directly into "the Dark Ages"—as many of us learned in school. The term "late antiquity" has replaced "the Dark Ages" in modern scholarship, and signals the intent of scholars to understand this period in its own terms, without the prejudice contained in the original term.

In recent years, John Boswell published his own account of this era: *Christianity, Social Tolerance, and Homosexuality* was, to a significant extent, a re-examination of the question of Christian intolerance of homosexuality. Boswell propounded a general argument that the Christian religion had little or nothing to do with the rise of sexual intolerance in late antiquity. Indeed, he seemed to argue that there was no such rise at all; that, if there was any such rise, it was slight; and that the cause of any such rise should be sought in factors (such as demographics) unrelated to Christianity.

The reader should have a chance to view the evidence for himself. Both Gibbon and Boswell seem to be biased authors—Gibbon shared the anti-religious bias of the Enlightenment and seems to have detested "sodomites" as well, while Boswell appears to be, at least to some extent, an apologist for both "gay people" and the Catholic church, differing from Gibbon on both issues.

As a result, we have a curious flaw in the published accounts of the rise of sexual intolerance in the Western world. Gibbon ignores the story as much as possible, and, where he cannot ignore it, laces his discussion with pejorative and condescending epithets. Boswell treats the subject at great length, and he appears to be comprehensive in his survey, but his piety often blinds him. There appears to be a need to review what actually happened, what was actually written, who did what, and to whom.

The central event discussed in the present work is the rise of Christianity in the Western world, and the often-ignored catastrophes that accompanied its triumph. The "candid mind" of Gibbon's time was frequently surprised when studying the deeds of this era; the skeptical mind of the twenty-first century is more often dumbfounded. In the time between the birth of Christ (circa 4 BC) and the year 500 AD, we find the triumph of Christianity and—simultaneously—the triumph of homophobia, religious intolerance, fanaticism, barbarism and the fatally anti-scientific attitude that did much to create the mental attitudes of late antiquity. Many other factors were involved: the barbarism of the northern Europeans and the rise of Islam cannot be overlooked, but the practices and teachings of the early Christian church were of central importance in this transformation. Before the rise of Christianity, the world was a place of paganism (however unfortunate that term may be), of a science which the Greeks were trying to nurture past infancy, and of a surprising tolerance for some forms of homosexual relations. After the rise of Christianity, paganism was banned, science was classed with magic and forbidden to all, and no forms of sexual behavior outside Christian marriage were permitted.

There seems little doubt that the early Christian revolution, like the Marxist revolutions of our own century, was accompanied by a host of good intentions, but the law of unintended consequences has dealt with these good intentions in its usual merciless way.

Although the rise of sexual intolerance has been overlooked by other authors, a closer study will be attempted here. Recent decades have seen a number of efforts to uncover the history of gay men, and this study joins these efforts in an attempt to piece together what may be the most important piece of gay history known to us. It is an error to look upon the "pagan" days as a lost sexual paradise, but nonetheless it seems clear that something important was lost during the transition to late antiquity. As we shall see later on, it was not only gay men who suffered during this transition; the anti-sexual program of the early Christian church was very broad, and initially frowned upon marriage itself. Female victims of rape were not consoled for their misfortune, but were blamed and disowned; eloping couples were liable to extraordinary punishments; and nurses could be punished by having boiling lead poured down their throats, if they made an error while guarding the virgin daughters of the Christian rulers.

Gibbon perceived these years as simple disaster: the Western Roman Empire fell; the knowledge built up during Græco-Roman antiquity was dissipated, and replaced by European barbarism; the people of Europe forgot how to read and write, and they forgot that the world was round.[1] The Eastern Empire did not fall, but gathered its jewels, elaborated its mysticism, and, tragically, did not preserve the intellectual heritage of the very regions it continued to govern.

I use the word "homosexual" with reluctance, and would prefer *erastes*, *eromenos*, *bachebaz*, or many other terms used by non-Christian cultures. I will try to avoid the word "gay." This word turns out, upon close examination, to be even more demeaning than "homosexual," although it has some advantage in avoiding the layers of psychiatric stigma that have accrued to the latter term.[2] Recent years have seen an attempt to revive the word "homophile," and I think that this has some merit, indicating that members of the same sex can and do love one another.

Accuracy demands that the dominant form of "Greek homosexuality" be referred to by its Greek name, pederasty (*paiderasteia* = "the love of boys"). There were other varieties of homoerotic behavior in Greece, but pederasty was the cultural and social norm. Labelling Greek behavior as "homosexuality" can be misleading, especially if it invites confusion with modern androphilia.

---

1. The shape of the world was known to ancient Greek mathematicians and scientists. Whether this fact was ever really forgotten is open to dispute, but medieval manuscripts frequently display an idealized flat earth. This may not have been a symptom of ignorance as much as indifference.

2. For a thorough investigation of both terms, see Dynes, Wayne R.: Homolexis (New York, 1985), or the discussions in the Encyclopedia of Homosexuality (New York, 1990). "Homosexual" (same-sex) is a term coined in the late nineteenth century. As an umbrella term which conceptually unifies all of the "same-sex" behavior known to the Greeks and the Romans (including pederasty, lesbianism, and many other varieties of behavior) it is an anachronism when used to describe Greek or Roman attitudes to sexual behavior.

It should be realized at the outset that the Jew, the Christian, and the "homosexual" constitute a genealogy in the history of ideas. Just as the Jew brought forth the Christian (and there could have been no Christians without the preceding Hebrew faith), so the Christian world eventually gave birth to the concept of the "homosexual." The concept and the term do not (or did not) exist in non-Christian societies.

The earlier societies had a large vocabulary for sexual acts and practices, of course. What appears to have happened, after Christianity established its religious hegemony, is that all activities between males were subsumed under the term of "sodomy" (which was used for a bewildering variety of other things as well) and then finally under the classification of "things which are not to be named in decent society." As a result of this systematic linguistic impoverishment, gay men found themselves without terms to describe themselves, and the struggle to find names for their sexual desires began with an attempt to create a neutral equivalent of sodomy—"homosexuality." As time goes on, it becomes apparent how much variety can be found under this umbrella term, and it also seems clear that the term was coined as a perhaps-unwitting reflection of Christian hostility—hostility to sexuality in general and to homosexuality in particular.

The story of this singular evolution begins in ancient Greece.

Paideia and Pederasty

Ancient Greece was the foundation of western civilization. Historical scholarship, with rare unanimity, declares this innovatory role to be a fact: the history of modern man begins in Greece. There, the twin lights of democracy and science first shone.

The earlier, eastern cradles of civilization were theocracies, characterized by the absolute rule of a priest-king and his priesthood. These societies were marked by a dogmatic rigidity which endured for thousands of years with little change and little progress. It could be argued, indeed, that the rulers of Sumer and Egypt found change threatening, and lacked the very concept of progress.

Against this vast, alien backdrop, the Greeks appear astonishingly modern. They explored the universe with joy and exuberance. An entirely new set of rules for living appeared, and the priestly classes were relegated to a more decorative role. The science of physics was born. Philosophy was born.

The traces lie in our language. Here is a list of Greek words for things very much with us today; the Greeks did not originate all of these, but they brought them to their first maturity: schools, gymnasiums, arithmetic, geometry, history, rhetoric, physics, biology, anatomy, hygiene, therapy, cosmetics, poetry, music, tragedy, comedy, philosophy, theology, agnosticism, skepticism, stoicism, epicureanism, ethics, politics, idealism, tyranny, plutocracy, and democracy.[3]

The Greeks made a profound advance in human civilization. Though many criticisms have been made of ancient Greek society, it is not possible to find another beginning to the history of western civilization.

One more word belongs on the daunting list above. It was formerly as noble as any of them, but is infamous in modern times—the word, of course, is pederasty.

Pederasty is a Greek word which means "the love of male youths or boys." The Greeks had no word—and no concept—which corresponds to our "homosexual." There is, now, no doubt that pederasty was common among the Greeks. Many commentators down to the present have tried to cover this up, or have even denied it altogether, but the evidence from ancient Greece is overwhelming. Professional historians have never really been in doubt: both Gibbon and Durant remark on the prevalence of pederasty, although they make sure to register their disapproval and incorporate in their remarks an uncommon number of errors—Durant, for example, follows Gibbon's mistake in asserting that Athenian law disenfranchised those who received homosexual attentions.[4]

Pederasty was sometimes evidence of the Greek love of pleasure, but its main purpose was education and social integration. The late Dr. Marrou

---

3. Durant, Will: *The Life of Greece*, p. vii (New York, undated).
4. Durant, p. 301. Gibbon's error occurs in *Decline and Fall*, volume 4, chapter 4, pp. 535-537, in his discussion of the anti-homosexual legislation of Justinian, and stems from a misreading of the oration of Aeschines against Timarchus, a text clarified by Dover.

was one of the few modern scholars who had the clarity of vision to recognize that pederasty and *paideia*[5] were inseparable in Greek culture.

> The Jews of the time of the Maccabees,[6] and the ancient Romans, were right in thinking that pederasty, like the athletic nudity with which it was closely connected, was one of the distinguishing marks of Hellenism—one of the practices in which it contrasted most sharply with the "barbarians," and hence in its own eyes one of the privileges establishing the nobility of civilized man.

> Although no mention of pederasty seems to occur in Homer, I do not think we need hesitate to trace it back to quite early times. It was bound up with the genuine Hellenic tradition as a whole; German scholarship is mistaken in regarding it, as it frequently does, as a peculiarity confined to the Dorian race.[7] In actual fact we encounter it quite as much elsewhere....

> The Greek type of love helped to create the particular kind of moral ideal that underlay the whole system of Hellenic education....The elder's desire to stand out in the eyes of his beloved, to shine, and the younger man's corresponding desire to show

---

5. *Paideia* is a Greek term for the education and training of children.

6. The Jews just before the time of Christ, that is, during the period when they were colonized by the Greeks; this period is discussed in the chapter below: "Jew and Greek in Conflict."

7. The Dorians were a later wave of Greek invaders.

himself worthy of his lover, could not but strengthen in both that love of glory which was, moreover, extolled by the whole agonistic outlook....The tradition of antiquity is unanimous in linking the practice of pederasty with valour and courage.[8]

As we develop a true picture of the role of pederasty in Greek civilization, it may startle us. The erotic love of a mature man for a youth or a boy (Marrou places the age of the youth between fifteen and nineteen) was a pillar of Greek education, and, for any society, education is the main building block for all further social development, the means by which its culture is transmitted. It is difficult to step back and realize that what many today call the "abominable crime against nature" was an honorable institution of ancient Greek society. Modern democratic societies have worked their way around to tolerating, more or less, "homosexual relations between consenting adults." But this is not what the Greeks admired.

The cultural difference is great: while we may admire the achievements of the Greeks and even feel indebted to them, there is, in their culture, a large and apparently central area of athletic nudity, pederasty, and celebration of masculine virtues which we simply do not comprehend.

---

8. Marrou, H. I.: *A History of Education in Antiquity* (trans. George Lamb), pp. 50–54 (Mentor edition, New York, 1964).

One way out of this dilemma is to ignore the Greeks. This has been done, usually with comments that the Greeks were a slave society (or an anti-feminist society) and, therefore, far from ideal.

These complaints are surely valid but do not really serve to distinguish the Greeks from the rest of the ancient world. The Biblical Hebrews, for example, were also a slave society. The Tenth Commandment (rendered as "Thou shalt not covet thy neighbor's maidservant") actually reads "Thou shalt not covet thy neighbor's female slave," and the modern commandment not to covet other men's "wives" actually refers to "women," since the Biblical Hebrew was allowed to marry as many women as he could buy.

On the other hand, the complex and intertwined area of athletic nudity, the love of youths, and the agonistic ideal, do seem to distinguish the Greeks from other ancient societies. The Greeks themselves were aware of this distinction and proud of it.

If the roots of Greek pederasty were located in some rudimentary theory of education, we may be faced with an institution which goes back to the mists of prehistory.[9] Vanggaard argues this case,[10] and it is perhaps easier to explain the prevalence of the custom if one postulates such an ancestry, and also easier to understand its respectability, to us seemingly inexplicable.

---

9. On this general topic, see Bernard Sergent's *Homosexuality in Greek Myth* (Boston, 1986).

10. Vanggaard, Thorkild: *Phallos* (New York, 1972).

Just how prevalent pederasty really was among the Greeks has long been disputed. Those who would impose our own morality upon the Greeks have, for many years, attempted to confine what they perceive as an abomination within very narrow borders. Thus Arno Karlen claims that only a "tiny literate minority" was involved, a "minority even in the Greek upper classes."[11] Some homosexual apologists would have us believe that all the Greeks were engaged in pederastic love affairs all the time, which is just as untenable.

The tide seems to be in favor of the apologists, however: the modern scrutiny of the Greek record, which takes place without the censorship and bowdlerism so long prevalent in classical studies, only strengthens our impression of how widespread the custom was.

But the main outlines have been known for a long time, and have even been incorporated into popular fiction. Mary Renault's novels show abundant evidence of thorough and impartial scholarship,[12] and rank well above many nonfiction polemics as an imaginative recreation of the world of Hellas. In *The Last of the Wine*, for example, we see Greeks who treat *eros* (erotic or romantic love) similarly, whether heterosexual or homosexual. Socrates and Plato are persuasively drawn, as is Xenophon, the latter having no use for the love of youths and thinking it perhaps unseemly.

---

11. Karlen, Arno: "Homosexuality in History," in Marmor, Judd: *Homosexual Behavior: A Modern Reappraisal*, p. 80 (New York, 1980).

12. The reader who is predisposed to dismiss all historical novels as worthless may wish to consult Bernard F. Dick's full-length study, *The Hellenism of Mary Renault* (Crosscurrents; Southern Illinois University Press, 1972).

The young male heroes, while deeply in love with one another, by no means ignore women or marriage.

The analysis and conclusions of K. J. Dover reinforce the picture given us by Mary Renault and the Platonic dialogues. Greek pederasty was an institution, an ancient custom, integral to the Greek way of life. It would be idle to claim that it was at any time illegal, although frowning puritans were not unknown. The walls of the Greek city-state were covered with homoerotic graffiti which might typically exclaim "Agathon is beautiful, or so it seems to me." Harmodios and Aristogeiton (male lovers who assassinated a tyrant) were popular heroes. It was widely assumed that the Greek heroes Achilles and Patroclus were lovers (although Homer is silent). Common opinion declared that the great god Zeus descended from the heavens to seize the boy Ganymede and fetch him to Mount Olympus, to serve as his cupbearer and lover.

If we had to compare Greek pederasty to some American institution, we would have to choose something like football. Not everyone loves football; we even have stern moralists who think it should be abolished. But it would be folly to assert that football was the pastime of a "tiny literate minority." Football is part of the American way of life—beloved of some, detested by others, but indisputably there, and, for the average citizen, a source of national pride. To deny the centrality of pederasty in Greek and Hellenic civilization would be just as absurd.

SOCRATES AND PLATO

Socrates and Plato were two very different men. Socrates was the teacher, while Plato presents himself as merely the student and scribe of Socrates.

Socrates himself, although married, was a famous pederast, but remarkable among the men of Athens for insisting that the truest and noblest form of pederasty imposed chastity on the lovers. The Socratic view is spelled out clearly in the *Phædrus* and the *Symposium*.

It seems important to begin by establishing Socrates' homosexual desires in clear terms. The fact that Socrates favored chastity did not mean that his admiration was merely intellectual. An explicit description of Socrates' feelings has been preserved by Plato in his dialogue, the *Charmides*.

> [At the palæstra in Taureas, Socrates is warned of the approach of Charmides, a youth of legendary beauty. Socrates says:]
>
> Now you know, my friend, that I am not good at measuring, and in the presence of the beautiful I am like a measuring line without marks, for almost all young persons appear to be beautiful in my eyes. But at that moment, when I saw him, I confess that I was quite astonished at his beauty and stature. All the company seemed to be enamored of him. Amazement and confusion reigned when he entered, and a second troop of lovers followed behind him. That grown-up men like ourselves should have been affected in this way was not surprising, but I observed the boys

and saw that all of them, down to the very smallest, turned and looked at him, as if he had been a statue.

Chærephon called me and said, "What do you think of the young man, Socrates? Has he not a beautiful face?"

"Most beautiful," I said.

"But you would think nothing of his face," he replied, "if you could see his naked form; he is absolutely perfect."

And to this they all agreed....

And all the people in the palæstra crowded about us [Socrates and Charmides], and at that moment, my good friend, I caught a sight of the inwards of his garment, and took the flame. Then I could no longer contain myself....I felt that I had been overcome by a sort of wild-beast appetite.[13]

This certainly suggests that Socrates did not preach pederastic chastity from a lack of sexual desire.

---

13. Plato, The Collected Dialogues, Princeton, 1963. The citation is trans. Jowett, pp. 100–102 (English text), pp. 153–156 (Greek text).

What should perhaps be emphasized is that Socrates rejected sexual activity between man and boy as less good than a chaste love affair, for philosophical reasons which may or may not be valid.

This view, in the hands of the older Plato who composed the Laws, became a demand for legal proscription of homosexual activity. These severe views are not attributed to Socrates, but to an anonymous Athenian; they may be safely ascribed to Plato himself.[14]

The middle-of-the-road views expressed in the Republic, where carnal relations are condemned, but kisses and caresses permitted, may be allotted to Socrates or Plato as personal judgment dictates. The preponderance of scholarly opinion sees much more of the severe Plato here than of the mild and inquiring Socrates; some eminent Platonic scholars even refuse to admit the authenticity of the "Socrates" found in the Republic.

Thus we are left with a Socrates who devoted his life to wisdom and the love of boys,[15] and claimed that such love must be chaste to lead to the highest good, but never claimed that laws should be passed to enforce his idiosyncratic ideal.

Plato, in turn, seems to have been a pederast himself in his younger days. The following epigrams from *The Greek Anthology* are attributed to Plato with some reliability:

---

14. See, for example, Dover, K. J.: *Greek Homosexuality*, p. 153 (New York, 1980).

15. The use of the word "boy," it should be re-emphasized, does not refer to children, as is shown in the passage from the *Charmides*.

Aster

My star, star-gazing? If only I could be
The sky, with all those eyes to stare at you!

Aster

You were the morning star among the living:
But now in death your evening lights the dead.

Alexis

All I said was—Alexis is gorgeous. Now
Everyone stares, ogles him everywhere.
Dear heart, why show the dogs a bone? You'll care
Later. Remember? Phædros went that way too.

Sokrates to Agathon

Kissing Agathon, I found
My soul at my lips. Poor thing!
—It went there, hoping
To slip across.[16]

---

16. Translations by Peter Jay, in the Penguin edition of *The Greek Anthology*, p. 45. (New York, 1981). (7.669, 7.670, 7.100, 5,78).

Aster (Greek for "star"), Alexis, Phædros, and Agathon were all young men. Yet this same Plato finished his life insisting that the love of young men should be legally proscribed.

In short, we are presented with strange and contradictory evidence about these men.

It may be helpful at this point to distance ourselves from these two and consider them from a pair of larger perspectives. Let us first try to determine their relation to the average Greek, and, second, their relation to the Christian church.

In relation to the thoughts and practices of the average Greek, Socrates and Plato were atypical. The average Greek would have been unlikely to idealize a love affair which did not include sexual pleasure, since the category of *eros* includes it. The Greeks were hedonists; they did not reject the physical world. Aristophanes spoke for them when he put Socrates in the clouds, preaching of imaginary paradises and spouting nonsensical arguments at all comers. In their most disgraceful moment, the Athenians condemned Socrates to death for blasphemy and corruption of the youth.

In relation to Christianity, we should note that the Christian church has been fond of Socrates and Plato—particularly the latter, but also Socrates: the role of the martyr has traditionally had the sympathy of Christian thought. The church exerted its theological energy to include these two in the group of pre-Christian philosophers who had been precursors and encouragers of the divine revelation which was to occur after their physical death. Erasmus found it natural to write: "Saint

Socrates, pray for us."[17] Eminent theologians spent worrisome hours debating whether the "divine Socrates" was in heaven or hell; it was a perplexing affair.

Why did these two Greeks find favor in the eyes of the church? Some reasons are fairly clear. Within the dialogues of Plato, we find the following propositions stoutly defended:

1. that spirits exist
2. that divine revelation exists and is to be heeded by philosophers
3. that sex is evil
4. that books which oppose truth are to be condemned and destroyed
5. that unseemly music is to be censored and condemned
6. that democracy is an evil form of government
7. that freedom of thought is dangerous nonsense
8. that divinely inspired monarchy is the best form of government for mankind
9. that the gods of Greek paganism were wicked inventions of mankind
10. that this life is followed by a judgment in the afterlife, where sinners will be punished and the blessed shall be saved

---

17. Cited in Artz, Frederick B.: *The Mind of the Middle Ages*, p. 11 (Chicago, 1980, paperbound edition).

11. that a scientific knowledge of God is possible, and that errors on this subject shall be punished with death
12. that the ideal state shall prohibit all extramarital intercourse and all homosexual behavior [18]

Moreover, many of the early Christian theologians relied on Plato (*via* Philo of Alexandria) for their theories of the Trinity, and claimed that these theories were mere extensions of Plato's necessarily imperfect vision.[19]

Thus, although Socrates led an exemplary life in many respects, it becomes apparent that Socrates and Plato were the progenitors, at least in

---

18. The following sub-notes deal with each point.
   1) Socrates' daimon is foremost among many.
   2) Socrates' theory of the divine madness is outlined in the *Phædrus*, particularly 244.
   3) *Phædrus* 253-255.
   4) *Republic*, Book 10 is enough in itself.
   5) *Republic* 397b-d is just one of many possible citations.
   6) *Republic* 560d etc.
   7) *Republic* 473c–e, *Republic* 498b–e, *Laws* 634d–c; also implied by items 4 and 5.
   8) What else is the philosopher king?
   9) many citations could be given; Socrates was condemned for this crime. See *Timæus, Republic*, etc..
   10) *Phædrus* 249a; *Republic* 614–615.
   11) *Laws*, esp. Books VII (821–822), XI (908–909) and XII (957–958).
   12) *Laws*, 841d–e.

An excellent source for Plato's totalitarian dogmas (but not for his religious absolutism) is Popper, who defends the innocence of Socrates and also claims that toleration and freedom of conscience are Christian doctrines, "at least as it is usually understood in democratic countries." This value-judgment is clearly not applicable to the early church.

19. Gibbon, vol. ii, chap. 21, p. 356 has several secondary citations; the ultimate reference is the *Timæus*.

part, of important Christian teachings which were to have a profound and largely malign influence on later generations. They rejected, finally, the real world and free inquiry into its nature. They were, in this respect, opposed to the Greek genius which is admired today, and it was in precisely this respect that they were admired by the early church, which has preserved their books for two thousand years.

Early Christians admired Socrates and Plato. The average Greek may have been less impressed.

Frederick B. Artz agrees that Socrates revolutionized Greek thought. The Greek mind, following Socrates' lead, began to turn away from the natural world, the world of *physis* (nature), and to turn towards study of an Absolute, a final perfection towards which all nature aspires. Artz points out that the effect on science "was, in the long run, disastrous."[20]

In the end, Socrates seems a melancholy figure. In the speech of Diotima,[21] he made pederasty the stepping-stone to divine wisdom: from the love of young men (properly understood), we progress to an understanding of the nature of beauty, and from there to still higher levels of wisdom. The average Greek paid no attention to his pederasty but found Socrates' chastity and "ideal beauty" to be unfamiliar territory. The church adopted the unfamiliar territory with enthusiasm, but was shocked by his professions of homoerotic love. Universally acknowledged as the father of

---

20. Artz, p. 12.
21. *Symposium* 211b.

philosophy, he seems to have been genuinely understood and respected by very few (least of them Plato), and then only during the brief twilight of the Hellenistic world.

Plato, upon consideration, assumes a more sinister mien, and seems worthy of the censure of judicious minds. It is not difficult to see that the totalitarian state envisioned in Plato's *Laws* would have condemned Socrates to death without hesitation. This development on the part of Plato is due to his theoretical World of Ideas, and his historical theory that all change is decadence. The goal of Plato's state was to arrest all change by forcing everyone to keep his place and think like a slave. His philosopher-king developed into a tyrant who employed propaganda and lies to keep the masses in their place. Plato ultimately defined justice as that condition where the rulers rule, the workers work, and the slaves slave.[22]

Intellectual treason is not too strong a term for what Plato did, though the charge is a grave one. Where Socrates inquired, patiently, of all the men in the city, was eager to instruct even slaves, and claimed that the beginning of wisdom was to admit that you knew nothing, Plato set himself up as a Man of Wisdom, possessing the keys to the Absolute, and began training others in the path of his Divine Wisdom. When he finally asserted that such an illuminated minority should assert a totalitarian rule over all other men, he sowed the seeds of at least two later disasters in

---

22. Popper, Karl: The Open Society and Its Enemies; Vol. I: Plato (Princeton,1971).

world history.[23] This is even more deplorable when we recall that he was fortunate enough to have had Socrates for his teacher. The student of the Athenian gadfly wound up training at least nine disreputable aristocratic tyrants, who were convinced that the Ideal State had no room for gadflies.

E. R. Dodds is another judicious scholar who agrees with this harsh assessment; he sums up Plato's political plan as follows:

1. He would provide religious faith with a logical foundation by proving certain basic propositions.
2. He would give it a legal foundation by incorporating these propositions in an unalterable legal code, and imposing legal penalties on any person propagating disbelief in them.
3. He would give it an educational foundation by making the basic propositions a compulsory subject of instruction for all children.
4. He would give it a social foundation by promoting an intimate union of religious and civic life at all levels—as we should phrase it, a union of church and state.[24]

This is a fair description of what was yet to come. We must note, in addition, that Plato was prepared to enforce the first item, above, by

---

23. Such thinking is highly congenial not only to the sort of Christians who favored the Spanish Inquisition, but also to Marxists of the Leninist tradition.
24. Dodds, E.R.: *The Greeks and the Irrational*, p. 219.

propaganda and lies, if he could not succeed in logically proving the necessary religious principles. This stratagem, as well, has often been employed by theocrats and other totalitarians.

ARISTOTLE

Unfortunately, most of the writings of Aristotle perished during the early Christian era. The library of Alexandria once held several hundred manuscript rolls by this philosopher, but we no longer have them.

What survives are notes from Aristotle's lectures, and fragments of the lost books scattered in the works of other authors. This corpus fits handily into two volumes, but its interpretation is difficult.

Aristotle did not make many references to pederasty and homosexuality. Perhaps he was indifferent to such loves, and touched on them only in passing. Confusingly, however, there is a Greek tradition concerning Aristotle's own pederastic loves.[25]

---

25. Buffière, Félix: *Éros Adolescent*, p. 159 (Paris, Société d'Édition "Les Belles Lettres," 1980) provides several ancient citations.

In the *Politics*, we have a few sentences. In 1262 Aristotle criticizes Plato's suggestion (in the *Republic*) that his philosopher-kings should hold all women in common. Aristotle objects that this scheme would leave the door open for offenses against the family—that is, offenses against the Greek idea of natural piety. As Aristotle remarks, "Other difficulties…will be assaults and homicides,…quarrels and slanders, all of which are most unholy acts when committed against fathers and mothers and near relations, but not equally unholy when there is no relationship."[26] He then takes up the potential problem of pederastic relations being similarly contaminated:

> Again, how strange it is that Socrates, after having made the children common, should hinder lovers from carnal intercourse only, but should permit love and familiarities between father and son or between brother and brother, than which nothing can be more unseemly, since even without them love of this sort [*i.e.* incestuous] is improper.[27]

Also in the *Politics*, 1269b 25-26, Aristotle takes up the question of the liberty of Spartan women. He believes that such liberty will inevitably lead to citizens being dominated by their wives and the desire for wealth, but he notes exceptions to his rule: "the Celts, and a few others who openly approve of male homosexuality."

This is a neutral observation made in passing, but also a strange one, since by all accounts the Spartans themselves were one of the "few others."

---

26. *Politics*, 1262a 25-30. (*The Complete Works of Aristotle*, ed. Jonathan Barnes, Revised Oxford Translation, Princeton, 1984, p. 2003).

27. *Politics*, 1262a 32-37 (p. 2003).

However, we are dealing with lecture notes, and we cannot expect perfect consistency from such a source.

In 1272 Aristotle informs us that the correctness of encouraging homosexual relations, as the Cretans allegedly did for reasons of population control, is a subject "which I shall have an opportunity of considering at another time." Elsewhere in the *Politics*, Aristotle describes tyrants who have been overthrown by homosexual lovers.

Our only other Aristotelian source is the *Nichomachean Ethics*, which can be confusing, since there are two discussions which appear somewhat contradictory.

In Book VIII, under the topic of friendship, the typical lover-beloved relationship makes a brief appearance as an inferior type of friendship. If we read this passage within the context of ancient Greece (the older male is the lover, aroused by the youth's beauty; the youth is providing pleasure for his lover but obtains no pleasure himself) then this passage seems fairly clear:

> For these do not take pleasure in the same things, but the one [the elder] in seeing the beloved, and the other in receiving attentions from his lover; and when the bloom of youth is passing the friendship sometimes passes too (for the one finds no pleasure in the sight of the other, and the other gets no attentions from the first); but many lovers on the other hand are constant, if familiarity has led them to love each other's characters, these being alike.[28]

---

28. *Nichomachean Ethics*, 1157a 5-15 (p. 1828).

The remaining passage in this book has been a source of trouble, principally because it seems hard to reconcile with the calm discussion just cited. I believe it can be made clearer, however, if we attempt to read it in the Greek cultural context.

Again, it is essential to realize that the boy in the pederastic relationship was not expected to find pleasure in his passive role.[29] Another sort of fellow entirely was the man who loves to play the passive role, and does it as often as he can throughout his life.

Such a division corresponds to what we find in Arab and Persian societies today—despite the bizarre excesses of the modern theocracy in Persia—where the pederast or *bachebaz* is simply the average Iranian male in one of his aspects, but the conspicuous adult male passive (Tunisian Arabic *hisan*; Farsi *kyuniyy*) is a figure of ridicule and, for boors, a target of abuse. This type of homosexual man was also singled out by the Greeks. He represented the sort of homoeroticism which was not approved and not viewed as normal. Unlike the men and boys involved in pederastic relationships, this sort of man was marginalized and stigmatized.

Putting the same thing in another way: if we accept the homosexual "radical" in all men (as suggested by Vanggaard, and confirmed by Kinsey, when he discovered that fifty percent of all American males would admit to either

---

29. The erotic art preserved on Greek vase paintings indicates that the approved mode of sexual intercourse in a proper pederastic relationship was intercrural ("between the thighs"), with the older partner taking the active role.

homosexual experience or desire,[30] then one may well wonder how many men are actually or potentially attracted to adolescent males, and—given the appropriate cultural conditioning, plus the daily sight of naked youths in the gymnasia—would be inclined to form erotic and educational friendships with them. Perhaps ancient Greece answers our question: a larger number than the current received wisdom would seem to predict. In any case, such relationships fell within the Greek range of "normal and approved." The adult male pathic did not, especially when he was conspicuous or promiscuous.

This may help to clarify the other passage in the *Nichomachean Ethics*. Aristotle is discussing pleasure, and the strange pleasures that may arise from habit or from a bad nature. He cites fingernail-biting as an example of a strange pleasure, and then mentions "the of sexual intercourse for males [sic]." As Dover points out,[31] the wording is strange and cannot be translated as pederasty or homosexuality.

I would suggest that Aristotle was referring to the "pathic" type and wondered why some men would find pleasure in an activity which leaves most men indifferent or worse. Aristotle continues that the pleasure may "arise in some by nature and in others, as in those who have been the victims of lust from childhood, from habit."[32]

Thus we find our general view of Greek society confirmed by the few surviving bits of Aristotle. It may be pointed out that some earlier authors

---

30. A more recent and surprising finding is that *heterosexual* men show a measurable sexual arousal when shown photographs of adolescent male buttocks, though the arousal is slight and the men claim to be unaware of it. See Weinrich, James D.: *Sexual Landscapes*, pp. 49-51 (New York, 1987). Perhaps Brongersma does not exaggerate when he claims that "the naked body of a beautiful boy radiates a kind of exciting sexiness perceptible by every normal man." (Brongersma, Dr. Edward: *Loving Boys*, p. 67, The Netherlands and New York, 1986.)

31. Dover, K. J.: *Greek Homosexuality*, p. 168 (New York, 1978).

32. *Nichomachean Ethics*, 1148b 25-30 (p. 1815). Note again that "pæderasty" is, in this passage, a mistranslation.

have claimed that Aristotle condemned all male homophilia as an unnatural or brutal pleasure by citing the passage above: it would seem that such authors have not paid sufficient attention to the text and the context in which it was written.

We should, however, note two aspects of Aristotle which will become more important as this history continues.

First, Aristotle became an important source to all later science. And he did claim, in the passage just cited, that the passive adult male homosexual must become that way by nature or by training, and that if it was by "nature," it was a bad nature. This was to fructify in the following centuries into a disease theory of homosexuality. This theory was to have significant influence on the later pagan tradition, but almost none on the Christian tradition which was to supplant it. The Aristotelian model merely codified the Greek construction of social reality in a "scientific" framework: pederasty was commonplace and normal, but the "effeminate man" was not.

This ideological schema provided an underpinning for centuries of medical tradition: the treatises of the Greek physician Soranus (*fl. c.* 120 AD) are lost, but a fairly liberal translation into Latin by Cælius Aurelianus (c. 500 AD?) survives. Book IX of Cælius' *Chronic Diseases* is entitled "On Effeminate Men or Pathics," and continues the Aristotelian discussion on the possible cause of homosexuality: it may arise from a "corrupt and debased mind," or it may be due to a "circumstance at conception," or it may be "an inherited disease."[33]

---

33. Cælius Aurelianus, *On Acute Diseases and On Chronic Diseases*, trans. I. E. Drabkin, pp. 901-5, University of Chicago Press.

The second theme to follow is that Aristotle, for all his faults, used a philosophical method fundamentally different from that of Plato. To put it simplistically, Aristotle worked from the observation of particulars to the cautious presentation of generalities. The method of Plato was contrary: one had to seize the eternal verities (the Forms), and, once that had been accomplished, one could confidently generate comment about particulars *ad infinitum*.

The distinction is not absolute. It is broadly true to claim Aristotle as the founder of modern science and the scientific method; it is also true that this heroic scientist claimed that men and women had differing numbers of teeth, which argues for some careless observation on his part.

Nevertheless, the distinction of methods is real. The Aristotelian method finally developed into the scientific method, an indispensable tool of all modern societies. The Platonic method, some twenty centuries later, appears to have been more useful as a means of seizing control than as a means of ascertaining truth.

Plato was a valuable source to the early Christian church, which in turn neglected or destroyed the works of Aristotle—which had no real impact on western civilization until *c.* 1200 AD. At this point, Aristotle's "disease model" became available to Christian civilization, which deployed it as it saw fit (disregarding his methods, his tentativeness, and his context) against every form of same-sex behavior which came into view, including the pederasty which Aristotle simply took for granted.

Greece: the Evidence of Literature

Greek literature presents the same image of pederastic love as the other sources available for examination.

A more thorough review of the literature would only repeat what is already known to most scholars, so I will limit this discussion to three authors: Homer, Theognis, and Aristophanes.

*   *   *   *   *

The case of Homer is puzzling, because he is silent on the subject of pederasty between Achilles and Patroclus. This silence is variously explained.

Some claim that, since the first Greek author was a stranger to pederasty, the custom was therefore a fad of a later, more decadent era of Greek civilization. We may adopt the theory that pederasty was a custom of the invading Dorian tribes, unknown among the Ionian Greeks. This is Vanggaard's position, and it may be ultimately traced to German scholarship.[34] It seems

---

34. Vanggaard, p. 31 (note) following Jæger and Bethe.

to be discredited among modern scholars, as Professor Marrou pointed out above (in *Paideia and Pederasty*).[35]

A second explanation is that the relationship was clearly pederastic, and that we are simply overlooking what must have been obvious to the original archaic Greek audience.

A third option is that Achilles and Patroclus had been lovers in the past, and had maintained their friendship for many years beyond the initial passion. Aristotle has already pointed out that a long friendship may develop from the initial attraction, and Theocritus makes the same point: "You should become more kind…so that when you possess a manly beard, we'll be to one another like Achilles and his friend."[36]

But we may be blundering right past the correct explanation, which is that Homer did not describe Achilles and Patroclus as lovers because they weren't. Socrates makes this point in Xenophon's *Symposium*, and cites other heroic friends known to be chaste. Perhaps we have too great a tendency to view Greek culture as a simplified whole; understanding that two male friends were commonly lovers as well, we may rush to put other, more heterosexual types into this Procrustean bed. However, this theory is weakened by the fact that the opinion seems to have been Xenophon's, not Socrates'.

The apparent truth is complex, and amalgamates many of these partial truths, as W. M. Clarke has shown in his masterful summary of the evidence.

---

35. K. J. Dover also rejects the idea of a Dorian specialty.
36. Theocritus, Idyll XXIX, trans. Daryl Hine, in *Theocritus: Idylls and Epigrams* (New York, 1982), p. 105.

Most ancient writers and commentators assumed Achilles and Patroclus were lovers in every sense of the word. Why? They were well aware that Homer never expressly names the heroes' passion. (Alcibiades, too, in Plato's *Symposium*, never says precisely what it was he hoped to get from Socrates, but did not get; but no one, then or now, doubts what it was.) The sexual question is in any case irrelevant. It is clear from the language, precedents and dramatic developments of the *Iliad* that Achilles and Patroclus are not Homeric "friends" but are lovers from their hearts. Patroclus lives his life only in the life of Achilles; and is in turn the only human being more important to Achilles than himself, than his own life, his own ego, and honor. Æschines said it well: although Homer frequently writes of Achilles and Patroclus, "their love, and the name of their friendship he conceals; assuming that what goes beyond the limits of goodwill is obvious to the educated among his readers."[37]

Clarke also points out, in the *Odyssey*, an interesting parallelism which suggests a pederastic relationship. He notes that Nestor gives Telemachus his son Peisistratus as a bedmate, and the gift is described as follows:

---

37. Clarke, W. M.: "Achilles and Patroclus in Love," in *Hermes*, 106, pp. 381-96 (1978).

And Nestor of Gerenia showed Telemakhos
under the echoing eastern entrance hall
to a fine bed near the bed of Peisistratos,
captain of spearmen, his unmarried son.
Then he lay down in his own inner chamber
Where his dear faithful wife had smoothed his bed.

He [Menelaus] said no more, but Helen called the maids
and sent them to make beds, with purple rugs
piled up, and sheets outspread, and fleecy
coverlets, in the porch inside the gate.
The girls went out with torches in their hands,
and presently a squire led the guests—
Telemakhos and Nestor's radiant son—
under the entrance colonnade, to bed.
Then deep in the great mansion, in his chamber,
Menelaos went to rest, and Helen,
Queenly in her long gown, lay beside him.[38]

---

38. Homer, *Odyssey*, Book III (see Clarke also).

Clarke also demonstrates that Thetis quite bluntly tells Achilles (after the death of Patroclus): "It is good to have sexual relations, and I mean with a woman."

The relationship between Achilles and Patroclus is, according to Clarke's careful reading, not a stereotype. Patroclus is older, and he is weaker. Achilles is the younger hero. It is not the classical pederastic relationship, and it is not the same as companionship (*hetairos*). What then is it? The answer, not too surprising, is love.[39]

*   *   *   *   *

Theognis is another interesting case. It seems to have been the verses of Theognis, more than anything else, which pushed Jæger into the realization that Greek pederasty was an ancient institution, intimately connected with education.

Theognis was a poet of the old, aristocrat-warrior class, conservative to his bones. The verses he left were addressed to his beloved, Cyrnus. The work is of special interest because he wrote in early times.

This elegiac poet is generally dated from the late sixth century, but may well represent a much older tradition. (Current scholarship tends to assess these lyrics as an amalgam of several writers which may take us well back into the time of Homer.)[40] His love poems to Cyrnus are much concerned

---

39. Licht, Hans (pseud. Paul Brandt): *Sexual Life in Ancient Greece* (New York, 1974) provides more information on Homer and his tradition.

40. Dover, p. 10.

with good breeding, and with Theognis' passion for Cyrnus. Less than 1,400 lines of Theognis are extant, yet these represent more than half of the surviving Greek elegiac poetry.

The general tone of these erotic and didactic elegies is established early on: "These things I tell you, Cyrnus, for your good; I learned them, as a boy, from gentlemen...."[41] The implication is that this is the teaching of the ancestors, again raising the possibility of an institution reaching back into Indo-European prehistory. A central part of this teaching was the emotion which bound Theognis to Cyrnus. In many places, this relationship is clear:

> As long as your cheek's so smooth, my boy, I won't
> Stop kissing you, you wouldn't even stop
> If the punishment for doing so were death.[42]

> That man is never happy who does not
> Love dogs and smooth-hooved horses and young men.[43]

---

41. Theognis, ll. 27-8, in *Hesiod and Theognis*, trans. Dorothea Wender (Penguin, 1976).
42. Theognis, ll. 1327-8.
43. Theognis, ll. 1265-6.

I wouldn't do you harm, my handsome boy,
Not even if the gods rewarded it.
I do not sit as a judge of petty crimes;
No handsome boys exist who haven't strayed.[44]

I give you wings. You'll soon be lifted up
Across the land, across the boundless crests
of ocean; where men dine and pass the cup,
You'll light there, on the lips of all the guests,
Where lithe, appealing lads will praise you, swelling
Their song to match the piper's sweet, shrill tone.
At length, my boy, you'll enter Hades' dwelling,
That black hole where departed spirits moan,
But even then your glory will not cease,
Your well-loved name will stay alive, unworn,
You'll skim across the mainland, over Greece,
Over the islands and the sea, not borne
by horses, Cyrnus, you'll be whirled along
by violet maids, the Muses; yours
Will be each practiced singer's finest song,

---

44. Theognis, ll. 1279-82.

As long as life exists and earth endures.
I give you this, for what? To be reviled—
To be betrayed and lied to, like a child.[45]

The praise of Cyrnus did outlive him, as Theognis promised. These verses were sung at the symposia of Athens, many years later.

> Clearly the book survived chiefly in aristocratic circles: not only the Theognidean pieces in it but many other poems too express a violent hatred for the *demos*, the commons, and we can best imagine them as sung by the aristocratic political clubs at Athens in Critias' time—in the circle which produced the Old Oligarch's pamphlet on the constitution of Athens, and to which Plato himself was closely allied by birth. Plato's own dialogue, [the *Symposium*], depicts the connexion of Eros and the symposium in its highest form; and that history is clearly reflected in the history of the Theognidea, for the loosely connected book of songs which appears as Book II of the collection is devoted to the praise of Eros, who was always worshipped at such gatherings.[46]

---

45. Theognis, ll. 237-54.
46. Jæger, p. 188.

In summary, Theognis is an authentic conservative voice, who says "Happy the lover who exercises, then goes home to sleep all day with a handsome boy."[47]

The German scholar Bethe made an interesting comment on pederasty: "The qualities of a man, his heroism, his *arete* [excellence or virtue], are in some way transmitted to the beloved boy through love. Therefore it is society's view that skilful and competent men ought to love boys; the state even exerts pressure on them to do so."[48]

For this idea, there is interesting cross-cultural evidence from a culture as far removed from the Greeks as possible: the tribes of Papua New Guinea. These tribes also have an organized system of man-boy sexuality. To take one tribe in particular: the "Sambia" initiate all males into the practice of passive fellatio at the age of seven or eight, which they continue to practice regularly until they reach puberty. At this point they switch roles and continue as the active partner until they reach the age of courtship and marriage.

The Greek idea of love seems nearly absent here, for the magical explanation does not require just one partner. These tribes believe that a little boy will not grow up into a proper man unless he gets regular dosages of

---

47. Theognis, ll. 1335-36.
48. Bethe, E.: *Die Dorische Knabenliebe*, p. 457, cited in Vanggaard p. 42.

semen from adult males. When the child reaches puberty, the magic has clearly worked, and it is now his turn to help the smaller ones in their development. (Other tribes in the area perform the magic via anal intercourse, but the idea is the same.)

There may be something similar at work with the Greek tradition (and in a hypothetical prehistoric Indo-European tradition). The emphasis is more individualistic, since a particular man selects a particular boy, and takes on the job of turning him into a man. In both cultures, this initiatory pederasty has a virilizing influence, and the resultant "proper man" will be able to take up the role of husband and father.[49]

At least we have some pointers in this direction, particularly the notion that the male virtue or *arete* is acquired through frequent copulation with an older man. As the Greeks advanced into written history, the preceding magical belief would have, by this account, receded, to be replaced by more intelligible theories of education.

The New Guinea tribes, by the way, offer a final possibility for the silence of Homer on the relations between Achilles and Patroclus. One of the most conspicuous features of the "Sambian" nightly homosexual rites is that they are a deeply kept *secret*—not just from outsiders, but from their own womenfolk.

---

49. The story of the "Sambia" is found in Herdt, Gilbert H.: *Guardians of the Flutes* (New York, 1981).

Dover suggests that the division of Book I from Book II in Theognis "was probably effected in the early Middle Ages, when sensibilities were jolted by the juxtaposition of extravagant expressions of homosexual emotion with stern exhortations to honesty and truthfulness." (Book II now contains most of the erotic material.) If so, this would merely be yet another example of Christian piety interfering with the transmission of classical Greek texts.

*   *   *   *   *

We close with Aristophanes. His picture of Socrates (in *The Clouds*) is funny, and touches on many of the themes under discussion. In one scene, we have a debate between "Philosophy" and "Sophistry," with the combatants dressed as fighting cocks. "Philosophy" is stern, puritan and conservative, while of course "Sophistry" is a flashy character with no redeeming virtues. As they join in battle, insults fly:

Sophistry: Your justice doesn't exist.

Philosophy: What? No Justice?

S: Then show it to me. Where is it?

P: Where is Justice? Why, in the Lap of the Gods.

S: In the Lap of the Gods? Then would you explain how Zeus escaped punishment after he imprisoned his father? The inconsistency is glaring.

P: Aaaagh. What nauseating twaddle. It turns my stomach.

S: Why, you Decrepitude. You Doddering Dotard!

P: Why, you Precocious Pederast! You Palpable Pervert![50]

To conclude from this that Aristophanes and all right-thinking Athenians despised pederasty is clearly wrong. In fact, "Philosophy" is simply the old moral order of Theognis dressed up in comic costume. The same figure who calls "Sophistry" a Palpable Pervert later delivers himself of a classic lament in favor of boy-love, a *Tristesse d'Olympio* of pederasty,[51] when he makes his principal speech.

> In the gymnasium too decorum was demanded.
> The boys were seated together, stripped to the skin, on the
>   bare ground,
> keeping their legs thrust forward, shyly screening their nakedness
> from the gaze of the curious. Why, so modest were students then,
> that when they rose, they carefully smoothed out the ground
>   beneath them,
> lest even a pair of naked buttocks leaving its trace in the sand
> should draw the eyes of desire. Anointing with oil was forbidden
> below the line of the navel, and consequently their genitals kept

---

50. Aristophanes (trans. William Arrowsmith): *The Clouds*, p. 82 (Mentor edition, New York, undated).

51. This phrase originated with Proust's Baron de Charlus, commenting on the scene at the end of Balzac's *Lost Illusions*, where Jacques Collin halts his carriage to view the early home of the young Rastignac.

their boyish bloom intact and the quincelike freshness of youth. Toward their lovers their conduct was manly: you didn't see *them* mincing or strutting, or prostituting themselves with girlish voices or coy, provocative glances.[52]

Any resemblance between the Socrates of *The Clouds* and the Socrates presented in the Platonic dialogues is coincidental. At the end of the comedy, Socrates' outraged clients attack his "Thinkery" and burn it to the ground. While this is fair game in a comedy, the historical Socrates was in fact put to death by the Athenians, employing much the same reasoning: we don't like what you think, so we will put you to death. As this history progresses, such regrettable actions will become more frequent.

---

52. *Clouds*, p. 87.

GREECE: THE LEGAL POSITION

For a long while, scholars of the ancient Greeks made a puzzling error: while they admitted the prevalence of what we would term "homosexual behavior" among the Greeks, they also claimed that it was illegal: freeborn Greek citizens could be degraded from the rank of freeborn citizen for "homosexuality." This was the informed position of no less a scholar than Edward Gibbon, and many other scholars relied on his conclusion.

Given what we know about the Greeks, this seems implausible—that Theognis, for example, could have been relieved of his citizenship for kissing the sweet cheeks of Cyrnus.

This persistent and confusing error has only recently been cleared up, by the eminent K. J. Dover. The error stems from a misreading of the oration of Aiskhines against Timarkhos. The Athenian law actually provided that free Athenian citizens who *prostituted* themselves forfeited *some* of the rights and privileges of citizenship.

A law of Solon prohibited pederastic relations between freeborn and slave. Also forbidden were the procuring of free boys, rape, and hiring out one's own son or ward for sexual purposes. A citizen who prostituted himself became ineligible for elective office and other rights of citizenship.

These are all the Greek laws known to us.

The reader should be wary of the large amount of secondary literature already in print which contains errors on this subject. To take a random example, an author named Flacelière states with seeming authority that "pederasty was forbidden by law in most of the cities," and does not cite any source for this assertion.[53] A reliable guide to ancient Greece is *Sexual Life in Ancient Greece*, by "Hans Licht."[54]

---

53. Flacelière, Robert, trans. James Cleugh: *Love in Ancient Greece* (New York, 1962), p. 63.
54. Licht, Hans (pseud. Paul Brandt): *Sexual Life in Ancient Greece* (New York, 1974). See especially pp. 411-460.

THE WORLD OF ROME

Rome was a very different place from Greece, and in many ways less brilliant and idealistic. Nevertheless, valuable data can be gleaned from the study of Rome: its world was enormous, compared with the Greeks, and accounted for most of the world known to Western man at the time.

The Roman empire was based on brute military force. The Roman symbol of authority, the *fascine*, has come down to us in the word *fascist*, and the meaning has not changed much over two thousand years. The early Roman republic soon gave way to the early empire. In the third century AD, the reign of Diocletian—a crucial period of attempted resurrection and malign transformation—saw the installation of a complete, barefaced autocracy; all pretense of consulting the Roman Senate was dropped. The late empire, which began with Constantine and the establishment of Christianity, saw this autocracy reinforced by a new and vivid assertion of the divinity of the emperor, and gradually became a theocracy.

It is obvious that the Roman empire rested on force; all empires do. Nevertheless, distinctions can be made. The Roman attitude towards force was linked to their lust for power, a lust deified by the national authors. As a consequence, something bizarre arose as a characteristic of Roman culture: a public and near-universal love of cruelty, expressed openly in gladiatorial death-duels and other bloodthirsty spectacles. This seems very far from the Greeks, whose public spectacles were the Olympic games, and who attempted to bring what they felt to be a higher culture to the people they conquered. (The Romans made a similar pretense, but it would seem that the real goal of their conquest was the acquisition of slaves and tribute.)

In addition, the final deterioration of the Roman republic into a static theocracy takes us back to the Oriental states of earlier Mediterranean history, and thus may be said to represent a retrogression.

However, no one was conducting experiments in democracy when the Roman empire came to power, and there is much to be praised in the empire. The atmosphere of religious and sexual toleration is noteworthy: the religious toleration was not perfect by any means, not universal, but it was much better than what was to follow. The *pax Romana* or "Roman peace" was genuine, and it brought a blessed prosperity and tranquillity to the Mediterranean world for a few centuries—this is not an achievement to be despised, and it was made possible, in turn, by the Roman Law, Rome's own bequest to all following western civilizations, a law which was Rome's own transcendent denial of cruelty and the rule of force. The success of the "Five Good Emperors" does much to explain the fanatically pro-Roman attitude of the barbarian emperor Diocletian, and his immense, partially successful effort to save the empire. The process of "saving the empire" seems to have continued for another thousand years: such was, and is, the power of the idea of Rome.

It was the rule of force which finally undid the empire, by most accounts. The frontiers had to be defended; rebellions had to be quashed. The standing army grew to massive size, and gradually became the power broker in Roman politics. The clearest demonstration of this power came when the army actually auctioned off the position of emperor to the highest bidder. (The high bidder probably had no idea how short his reign was to be.) Having gained the seat of power, the army gradually extracted greater wages and "donatives" from the struggling emperors, and this led to the final demoralization and collapse. There were simply not enough taxpayers to support both the rapacious soldiers and the bureaucratic anthill which accompanied them and sometimes directed them. The nobles charged with collecting the taxes could not get them from the farmers—they had deserted their farms. In turn, these nobles were obliged to pay the taxes from their own pockets; when they understood their predicament, they deserted as well. The Western Empire, thus weakened, fell an easy prey to Germanic barbarians.

One of the redeeming Roman qualities was sexual toleration. The sexuality of the human male had fairly free play throughout the Empire, and by many contemporary accounts the female was not far behind. As in Greece, we find laws against rape, pimping of free citizens, and so forth, but no law against homosexual activity *per se*.

In the domain of homosexual behavior and pederasty, however, the Roman beliefs and practices were different from those of the Greeks. The noble Greek pederastic ideal was, for most Romans, a cultural pretension: something akin to a New Yorker donning a French beret. The homosexual affairs of the Roman citizen were not likely to follow the pederastic ideal; they were strictly affairs of romance and of *eros*. Roman history and literature provide us, it seems, with a few characters and people who seem not enormously different from modern homosexuals. The love of boys was widely known, but not central to the Roman ideal; the love of mature men ("androphilia") seems to assume a wider prominence.

In some ways, the Roman world may appear more sympathetic and hedonistic than that of the Greeks. Where the Greek would have fallen in love with a youth and had a great courtship and a great friendship, the Roman, on seeing a beautiful youth, was much more likely to try to copulate with him as soon as possible, disregarding philosophy entirely. The homosexual brothels of Rome were monuments to fleshly indulgence, and they did not begin with the political decadence of the later empire. The popular superstition that the late empire witnessed an unparalleled sexual laxity reverses the historical record. These brothels were only abolished in the very late empire, and the simplest indication that the Romans had no such thing as "a law against homosexuality" is that all the emperors regularly collected a tax on the revenues from these brothels, and the tax only ceased at the time these brothels were abolished.

What was new in Roman society was the widespread use of slaves for sexual purposes. Like most ancient peoples, the Romans had probably always practiced slavery. But the slaves of the peasant community were of necessity few. However, the successful conclusion of the Samnite, Punic and eastern Mediterranean wars brought in enormous influxes, sometimes as many as 25,000 in one day if ancient sources are to be believed.

By the end of the Roman republic in the first century of our era, slaves amounted to thirty or thirty-five per cent of Roman Italy, a figure quite close to that of the American Old South. The cheapness and abundance of this form of property clearly invited arbitrariness and maltreatment. Slaves were routinely beaten to relieve the frustrations of their masters and mistresses. Until the time of Hadrian, Roman law permitted their summary execution by their masters. For those with means, then, slaves were readily available and, once acquired, highly malleable.

Besides serving as targets for sadism, slaves were also objects of lust. As Seneca remarks: "Unchastity (*impudicitia*) is a crime in the freeborn, a necessity for a slave, a duty (*officium*) for the freedman."[55]

This common situation had an unfortunate result: homosexual relations in Greece were generally located in the idealized pederastic relationship, but in Rome they came to be found in non-consenting relations between master and slave. As early as the comedies of Plautus (died *c.* 184

---

55. Controversies IV, 10 cited in "Rome, Ancient" by Wayne R. Dynes in the *Encyclopedia of Homosexuality*, p. 1121 (New York, 1990).

BC), the master's lust for his slave boys is the chief homosexual element. In the poems of Horace (discussed below), it is clear that attractive slaves in the great houses of the rich were expected not only to cater to their master's lust, but to satisfy dinner guests as well.

In addition, it should be noted that the practical toleration of male homosexuality in the Roman empire coexisted with a great deal of Roman homophobia. The early Roman republic lacked the social institution of pederasty and, in fact, one searches in vain for any socially approved form of male homosexuality in those early days. Certainly, later orators and authors such as Cicero, Cato and Scipio referred to the early days of the republic as a sort of "Golden Age," where not only homosexual behavior but the taking of warm baths were regarded as unmanly and therefore un-Roman conduct.

Counterbalancing this manifest Roman tradition of pejoration is the appearance already in the first century BC of such eminent authors as Virgil, Ovid and Horace, all of whom discuss or depict homosexual passions with equanimity and impartiality. It is thus impossible to speak of "the" Roman attitude towards the subject.[56] What we are left with is extensive evidence of homosexual behavior in all visible social classes and the *de facto* toleration of such behavior (within certain limits, which persons such as Nero and Elagabalus exceeded).

---

56. MacMullen, Ramsay: "Roman Attitudes to Greek Love," *Historia*, 31 (1982), pp. 484-502 provides an excellent overview of negative attitudes towards homosexuality in Roman sources.

ROME: THE EVIDENCE OF LITERATURE

Roman literature provides a variety of viewpoints on sexual behavior. If a comparatively mainstream voice in the broad spectrum of Latin literature is wanted, Horace is probably as good a choice as any.

Horace (65-8 BC) lived through the civil wars which saw the Roman republic give way to the early empire, and he became Rome's most respected poet. He was considered an apostle of moderation and simplicity. He is funny and has some important things to say about greed and the simple life.

In Book I, Satire 2, Horace castigates his friend for lacking good sense in sexual matters; the friend is evidently much too fond of seducing married women. Horace emphasizes the dangers and the expense of this foolish course, and insists that sex is merely an appetite—not a master. Says the poet:

> Who hunts for golden cups when thirst strikes?
> Hungry, do you starve except for peacock
> And salmon? When passion afflicts you
> Would you rather do nothing, and suffer, than leap on

Some serving wench, some slave-boy, who happens
To be near? Not me: give me a mistress who gives in![57]

It is interesting that Horace makes no moral distinction between the choice of the girl or the boy. This may strike some modern minds as strange, and may also explain why this brief passage remained untranslated into English until recent times.[58]

There is something else in this passage which many will find morally or ethically objectionable for quite different reasons. "Have the slave boy, old chap!" may indeed be the creed of the Roman apostle of moderation, and following his advice may have made life uncomplicated for the slave-owner—but there is scant regard for the human needs of the slave in this scheme. Again, the cruelty of the Romans reappears as their besetting vice, the *hubris* which eventually brought them down. This widespread boy-raping, if indeed it was as widespread as it may have been. would have given pederasty a bad name, and would also have given the opposing camp (Roman ascetics and the early Christians) some valid arguments to use against the practice, arguments which they had rarely been given by the Greeks.

---

57. Horace (trans. Burton Raffel): *The Essential Horace*, Satires I, 2, p. 136 (San Francisco, 1983).
58. Rudd, Niall : *The Satires of Horace and Perseus*, p. 32 (Penguin, 1973).

Rome: the Legal Position

Did the Romans have a law opposing homosexual behavior?

The question itself seems questionable when the custom of collecting taxes from male brothels is recalled. Nevertheless, other writers have made claims about two Roman laws, the *Lex Scantinia* and the *Lex Julia de adulteriis*, so it seems essential to look at them.

The *Lex Scantinia* is frustrating. Secondary sources continue to cite it as a pristine ancient law which forbade sexual relations with a freeborn youth, or words to that effect. But even the name is ambiguous: it is spelled *Scatinia* and *Scantinia*. The text of the law does not survive: as Gibbon noted: "The name, the date, and the provisions of this law are equally doubtful." Vern Bullough remarks that "scholars are not now certain there ever was such a law."[59] Boswell also examines the scanty evidence and dismisses it.[60]

---

59. Bullough, Vern: *Sexual Variance in Society and History*, p. 137 (Chicago, 1981).

60. Boswell, pp. 65-69.

Three things about this law may be deduced. First, it was, purportedly, a law against sexual relations with a freeborn youth. It did not extend to slaves or adult males. Second, it may not have existed. Third, it was not a law which was long enforced, even if it did exist. These three elements may possibly point to an unwritten code among the ruling families of the early Republic, something similar to their abhorrence of warm baths, but this is only speculation.

For more speculation about this law, I refer the reader to the sources cited.

The *Lex Julia de adulteriis* is revealing, especially since it was the work of Augustus, an emperor often regarded as a prude. The law is only concerned with preventing heterosexual activity with prohibited women, neglecting the domain of homosexual activity entirely.[61]

There has been, as with the *Lex Scantinia*, a tradition of secondary sources claiming that there was some sort of anti-homosexual "law" contained in the *Lex Julia*. For some reason, these same secondary sources assume that homosexual behavior was illegal amongst the ancient Greeks.[62]

There has been a persistent search for anti-homosexual laws in Rome before the advent of Constantine and the Christian theocracy. The advantage of such a find is obvious: it would strongly imply that the Roman

---

61. Boswell, p. 70 *etc.*; Dynes, Wayne, personal communication.
62. Bullough's statement that the *Lex Julia* declared homosexual intercourse to be a *stuprum* (p. 138) appears problematic.

laws against homosexuality were not linked to any particular religion. The major hunt centers on some crypto-history in the third century AD.

When the dust settles over the unappealing spectacle of historians grasping at straws, a possibly factual account emerges: after the colorful (and notoriously homosexual) emperor Elagabalus was assassinated, the puritan Severus Alexander assumed the throne, and, according to the *Scriptores historiæ Augustæ* (*SHA*), "contemplated" outlawing male prostitution. A later emperor (Philip the Arab), during a period of chaos, is reported to have actually issued a law abolishing male prostitution, but the abolition was not effective. The only source for all of this is the obscure historian Aurelius Victor, who wrote his account *circa* 360 AD, generations after the death of everyone involved.

An interesting aspect of this series of non-events is that a typical historian might be tempted to say that the *SHA* confirm the testimony of Aurelius Victor, whereas in fact this "confirmation" is a key piece of evidence demonstrating that the *SHA* are a forgery.[63]

And so the entire attempt to find a pre-Christian law against homosexuality seems to fail. The two emperors mentioned were not typical Romans and may well have been crypto-Christians, the subject under debate was male prostitution, not homosexual behavior *per se*, and the entire story may be a fable.

---

63. On this point, see Syme, Sir Ronald: *Ammianus and the Historia Augusta* (Oxford, 1968).

No such difficulties arise with the text of the first Christian law against homosexual behavior. It deals with homosexual behavior in the most general sense, not with the subcategory of male prostitution. The date is unambiguously 342 AD, and the penalty is clear—death by beheading.[64]

So the picture seems clear enough. The Romans tolerated a wide range of sexual acts. They sensibly enforced the human rights of their citizens and, dangerously, ignored the human rights of their slaves. This policy of toleration, though limited to citizens and hedged about with various restrictions, went hand in hand with the Roman policy of religious toleration.

An Increase in Pagan Asceticism

Another development that seems clear is a rising puritanism among the pagan elements of the Roman empire. After all, even though Sextus Empiricus was wrong about the laws in Greece and Rome, the error may be instructive. The influence of the older Plato had spread through the ancient world, along with the "disease theory" of homosexuality suggested by Aristotle, and it is intriguing that Sextus Empiricus *felt* that homosexual behavior should have been illegal in Greece. The rejection of hedonism

---

64. See the full text in *The Conversion of Constantine,* below.

and sexual pleasure was quite widespread among pagan schools of philosophy: the Stoics and the Epicureans hardly disagreed on the subject. Such a rejection of the pleasure principle, some Freudian mystics speculate, may be linked to the civilization's unconscious death-wish.

The picture which I have drawn so far will now account for the Mediterranean world from at least 700 BC to approximately 200 AD. Somewhere near this point, an arbitrary historical watershed is reached: the transformation of the world of Greece and Rome into the world of late antiquity. For that reason, I would ask the reader to fix something in his mind: around the basin of the Mediterranean sea, in ancient Greece as well as Rome, men loved men and men loved boys with no legal penalty whatever, other than the common-sense measures against rape and coercion. Jokes were directed against the adult male passive, but he was not jailed. This ancient Mediterranean pattern was, in one respect, startlingly tolerant: one of the main patterns was love between men and adolescent youths. The Greeks did not tolerate sex with children, and one doubts that the Romans did either.[65] The young man or adolescent boy was a universal Greek and Roman ideal of beauty: the evidence of painting and sculpture is persuasive testimony of this fact. The emperor Hadrian, perhaps the best of all the emperors, devoted his heart and his life to his beloved Antinous, and is probably the most obvious pederast

---

65. Undoubtedly, Suetonius' revelation about Tiberius' "minnows" was meant to be especially damaging. (These "minnows," according to Suetonius, were sexually immature slave-boys who swam naked in Tiberius' swimming-pool, and were expected to fellate him on demand. The charge may or may not be true, but the intent to damage Tiberius' reputation is evident.)

in human history. When Antinous suddenly died, Hadrian went mad with grief and attempted to deify him. Statues of Antinous were erected all over the empire.

Strangely enough, the attempt to deify Antinous succeeded. There was an Antinous cult for several centuries, and devoted citizens offered sacrifice to the mysterious god whose unearthly beauty was limned in the severe marble. This may give one pause, as further evidence of what a small pretext may serve as the beginning of a religion.

However, in one corner of the Roman world, religious and sexual tolerance did not prevail. That corner was Palestine, and it is Palestine and the Jews which now demand our attention.

The Mosaic Tradition

YOU SHALL NOT LIE WITH A MAN AS WITH A WOMAN:
THAT IS AN ABOMINATION.

IF A MAN HAS INTERCOURSE WITH A MAN
AS WITH A WOMAN,
THEY BOTH COMMIT AN ABOMINATION.
THEY SHALL BE PUT TO DEATH;
THEIR BLOOD SHALL BE ON THEIR OWN HEADS.[66]

This portion of the Mosaic tradition on homosexual behavior is unambiguous, and violent.

---

66. Leviticus 18:22 and 20:13. (All Old Testament citations are from *The New English Bible* unless otherwise noted.)

These few sentences, written down long ago by an unknown hand, have been of incalculable importance to homosexual and bisexual men in western civilization: we cannot number the innocent victims of priests and kings since this prohibition was penned by an unknown Jewish scribe.

If there is a root of violent sexual intolerance in the western world, we are looking right at it. As we have seen, Plato and some other men of the Græco-Roman tradition were intolerant of homosexual behavior, but they were merely human. The unique import of the words of Leviticus is that they claim to be *the word of God*. The difference is crucial: opinion and taste vary from man to man; it is another case entirely when the most ancient sacred scriptures carry the divine message that *God hates homosexuals and wants you to kill them*.

For example, if you are faced with someone like Plato who advances the claim that homosexuality is "against nature" (*para phusin*),[67] you can always point out that no man models his behavior on nature. There is room for debate and discussion. If a holy man tells you that God hates homosexuals and wants them dead, the only recourse is to tell him that there must be something wrong with his books, which makes you an "unbeliever." This is not a great worry when the holy man is in the minority, but the situation is quite different when the machinery of government lies in his hands.

This extraordinarily important dogma has been downplayed for many years by Jewish and Christian apologists. The extreme feminist-lesbian

---

67. *Laws*, 636b-c, 835e-842.

Andrea Dworkin calls these proscriptions "shrewd and pragmatic."[68] She permits herself such chilling indifference because she is not worried about the fate of male homosexuals, only of lesbians. John Boswell also tries to downplay the importance of the dogma, on the grounds that the Council of Jerusalem (49 AD) had established the principle that the teachings of the Old Testament are not binding on Christians.

At first, the argument is plausible, even persuasive. But it falls of its own weight, simply because most Christians are not aware of this Council: most Christians know only that the "Holy Bible" is the "Word of God." To say that Christians do not hold the Old Testament sacred is, sadly, to say nonsense. (It even contradicts the teachings of Jesus.)[69] How many sermons have we not heard on the Ten Commandments? Did not the early church fathers, indeed the very authors of the gospels, pore constantly over the Old Testament to find the prophecies of Christ's coming?

The practical result of the Council of Jerusalem was not to legalize homosexuality for Christians: it freed gentile Christians from circumcision and the Jewish dietary rules. It vindicated St. Paul's claim that Christian converts did not have to become Jews before becoming Christians, and thereby gave Paul *carte blanche* to preach the gospel to the heathen. (The dissenting party at the Council was the original Church of Jerusalem, represented by the disciples and a brother of Jesus.)

Another argument often offered against Leviticus is that, quite simply, it is one of the least intelligent religious books ever written. Anyone who has looked into the book is likely to develop his own list of oddities in it.

---

68. Dworkin, Andrea: *Right-Wing Women* (New York, 1983).
69. Matthew 23: 2-3.

As one example among many, Leviticus forbids us to eat rabbits, but assures us that grasshoppers are fine to eat. It is a textbook example of priestly hair-splitting, and, for just that reason, is largely ignored today.

Unfortunately, this argument fails, because Leviticus has never been *completely* ignored. In the midst of a huge roster of laws of daily conduct so arbitrary as to seem incomprehensible, lies another, smaller roster of laws for sexual behavior. This smaller, coherent sexual code stands out as a separate entity, easily used on its own—just as the Ten Commandments stand out from the rest of the Old Testament. In particular, Leviticus 20: 10-20 contains precisely what was to become the sexual code of the Jews—and later, the Christians. So the argument of absurdity fails because the absurd parts of Leviticus have always been ignored (at least by Christians), but never the sexual code. The sexual regulations became part of Jewish secular law, and were written into Roman law when the Christians assumed power. A law against homosexual behavior, usually specifying the death penalty, was written into every lawbook which the Christian church ever gained influence over: into the laws of Europe, Latin America, and the North American colonies. All the plausible arguments of Dworkin and Boswell fade into insignificance when we open the lawbooks of Massachusetts and read: "If any man lyeth with mankinde, as he lyeth with a woeman, both of them have committed abhomination, they both shall be surely put to death. *Lev* 20:13." So enacted the pilgrim fathers in Massachusetts—as well as Connecticut, New Hampshire, New York, New Jersey, and Pennsylvania.[70]

---

70. Crompton, Louis: "Gay Genocide from Leviticus to Hitler" in Crew, Louie: *The Gay Academic* (Palm Springs, 1978), p. 71. According to Robert F. Oaks, "Defining Sodomy in Seventeeth-Century Massachusetts," *Journal of Homosexuality*, vol. 6, nos. 1/2, Fall/Winter 1980/81, the text of the *law itself* cited Leviticus.

This, it would seem, undoes the sophistries about the Council of Jerusalem, and also destroys the notion that the "naturally homophobic" people of western civilization went to Leviticus to find justifications for their homophobia.[71] The Council of Jerusalem did *not* free Christians from the laws of the Old Testament—it did not free them from the Ten Commandments and it did not free them from the sexual code of Leviticus. The idea that Europeans were "naturally homophobic" seems implausible when we search in vain for a pre-Christian law against homosexual behavior.

In fact, the most plausible explanation for the transformation in attitudes towards homoerotic behavior is also the oldest one: Christianity replaced paganism as the universal religion, and brought about significant changes in virtually every aspect of life. One of the most obvious transformations involved social attitudes towards homoerotic behavior, which was never acceptable to the Christian church in any form, and was indeed to become a paradigm of evil and of Satanic influence.

Christians went to Leviticus for a code of sexual conduct, and found one: a code hallowed by Jewish tradition and the name of God. Having found it, they passed it into law. The fact that the code contained dire penalties for gay men appears to be a piece of bad luck: had the anony-

---

71. This is another theory of Boswell's (p. 105): "Their extreme selectivity in approaching the huge corpus of Levitical law is clear evidence that it was not their respect for the law which created their hostility to homosexuality but their hostility to homosexuality which led them to retain a few passages from a law code largely discarded."

mous scribe not put them in, things might have been quite different during the next two or three thousand years.

Which leads to the question: how did the anti-homosexual sentences get into the sexual code of Leviticus?

After all, it is not obvious that the Jews had always considered homosexuality a capital crime. If it had been so very important an issue, it is hard to understand why the ten commandments fail to mention it. It is also hard to understand how the pious scribes could have continued copying down, over the centuries, the patently homoerotic love story of David and Jonathan.[72] Another clear difficulty is the survival of male homosexual temple prostitution in Israel well into historical times.

What seems probable is that this particular prohibition stems from Persian sources. As we shall see, the conquest of Israel and the consequent exile to Babylon were world-shattering events to the Biblical Jews. They were released from this exile by the Persians, who at that time proclaimed a Zoroastrian teaching which is the most homophobic known to modern scholarship:

> O Maker of the material world, thou Holy One! Who is the man who is a Dæva? [*dæva* is, roughly, "demon"] Ahura Mazda

---

72. The best account to date is Horner, Tom: *Jonathan Loved David* (Philadelphia, 1978).

answered: The man that lies with mankind as man lies with womankind, or as a woman lies with womankind, is the man that is a Dæva; this one is a man that is a worshipper of the Dævas, that is a male paramour of the Dævas, that is a she-Dæva; that is the man who in his inmost self is a Dæva, that is in his whole being a Dæva; this is the man that is a Dæva before he dies, and becomes one of the unseen Dævas after death: so is he, whether he has lain with mankind as mankind, or as womankind.[73]

As Horner points out, "a footnote on the same page in this translation says that the guilty 'may be killed by anyone without an order from the Dastur'—it was the only criminal offense of which this was true—'and by his execution an ordinary crime may be redeemed.'"[74]

The striking similarity between the wording of the Persian prohibition and the wording of Leviticus may give us an approximate date for the insertion of the anti-homosexual clauses into the sexual code of Leviticus: sometime after the Babylonian exile (587-539 BC) and during the "Persian period" of Jewish history (539-333 BC).

It was a time when ritual purity was becoming a very important matter to the Jews: before the Exile, the faith was not highly codified; after the Exile, "the kind of Judaism that was to be passed down to the Christian or Common Era was largely formulated."[75]

---

73. Horner, p. 78.
74. Horner, p. 78.
75. Horner, p. 79.

The Jews and the Persians were to undertake parallel struggles of purification: their enemies were the predecessor religions in each country. The Persians made war against a common prehistoric Indo-European paganism, while the Jews were concerned with the vast pagan temples of Ishtar and other gods and goddesses.

Having inserted this clause into the Holiness Book of Leviticus, the Jews adopted it as their own. They enforced it, and they preached it to the unclean. And, of course, they were convinced that they were the only people in the world who were in possession of the true religion.

The precise method for assuring that the blood of the transgressors should "be on their own head" was stoning to death. The Talmud describes the procedure:

> The place of stoning was twice a man's height. One of the witnesses pushed him by the hips, so that he was overturned on his heart. He was then turned on his back. If that caused his death, he had fulfilled his duty. But if not, the second witness took the stone [*i.e.* a heavy stone that it took two men to lift] and threw it on his chest. If he died thereby, he had done his duty. But if not he [the criminal] was stoned by all Israel, for it is written: the hand of the witnesses shall be first upon him to put him to death, and afterwards the hand of all the people.[76]

*   *   *   *   *

---

76. Crompton (in Crew), pp. 68-9.

The Levitical injunction was subsequently reinforced by an interesting development of the legend of Sodom.

The original legend, blunt and inelegant, is a curious piece of work. The inhabitants of Sodom attempt a homosexual gang-rape of the angels of God.[77] It would seem evident that this is not the way to behave if you wish to gain the favorable attention of God. The original legend, however, is significant because it does not single out the homosexual aspects of the crime for special attention, and neither do the various commentaries on it. The general crime was inhospitality, as shown by the brutish attempt at gang-rape; that is why God destroyed the town of Sodom. None of the language in the Old Testament suggests that God was particularly upset about the homosexual nature of the rape. And this is not surprising, since the Sodom legend predates the Persian additions to Leviticus.

However, once the Jews had adopted their definitive anti-homosexual position (after the Babylonian exile) the scribes and teachers went to work on the legend of Sodom with all the wisdom that hindsight usually provides. When the original legend was added to the Levitical prohibitions, there was no stopping the legend of Sodom. It was a favorite topic of religious discourse, and received a vast elaboration in the hands of the early Christian fathers. Eventually the term *sodomy* became one of the most difficult (or semantically iridescent) terms in the language, referring to many different categories of behavior which the speaker deemed evil (luxury, heterosexual brothels, and so on were all called "sodomy").

---

77. For some reason, Boswell fails to read the original story correctly, insisting that *yadha* is to be construed as "to know" rather than as "to copulate." (He is probably following the lead of Canon Bailey.) The parallel story in Judges 19 makes his attempt ridiculous, aside from the fact that "getting to know you" is not the sin of a violent crowd, and God's subsequent destruction of Sodom lacks any motive.

Hence, it becomes necessary to inquire into the precise meaning of the word whenever it occurs.

The Jews were not originally much different from their neighbors in the Middle East, as we can see from the phenomenon of male homosexual temple prostitutes.

THE KEDESHIM

The earliest mention of a personage resembling the *kedeshim* (that is, male homosexual temple prostitutes) occurs in the Code of Hammurabi. Law 187 states that "the [adopted] son of a chamberlain or the [adopted] son of an epicene shall not be [re]claimed."[78] The "epicene" is the troublesome term here. He/she is listed as one of the "women of religion," but does not seem to be quite simply a woman. In this law, the "epicene" is mentioned in the same passage as the chamberlain, who was a eunuch. The word translated as "epicene" is SAL-ZIKRUM, and the interpreters of the law state that "there is every reason to suppose that neither the chamberlain nor the SAL-ZIKRUM had natural children." They further note, with puzzlement, that the word seems to mean "man-woman."[79] This is hardly conclusive evidence, but if the SAL-ZIKRUM were analogous to the *kedeshim*, the data from the Middle East would retain consistency.

---

78. Driver, G. R. and Miles, John C.: *The Babylonian Laws* (Oxford, 1955), vol. ii, p. 75.
79. Driver and Miles, vol. i, pp. 367-68.

An expert in ancient Middle Eastern language and culture, working directly from primary sources (ancient cylinder seals), definitely establishes the presence of such male temple prostitution.

> The swarms of street women may have differed from the cult prostitutes only in not having other religious duties to perform, for they too were *ex officio* devotees of ISHTAR. As well as women, men "whose manhood ISHTAR has changed into womanhood" offered themselves. Odd allusions in literary texts allow a lurid picture to be painted of streets and gardens abounding with mating couples.[80]

Anal intercourse seems to have been standard practice with both male and female prostitutes—with the female to avoid pregnancy—so the male and female *kedeshim* seem to have offered very similar services.

The eminent Finnish researcher Westermarck is entirely in agreement.

> It is noteworthy that in some of the Semitic cults there was a prostitution of men....and it is known that male prostitutes were serving Ishtar at Erech. *Qedeshim* were attached to Canaanite temples. The word properly denotes men attached to a deity, but

---

80. Lambert, W. G.: "Morals in Ancient Mesopotamia," Van Het Vooraziatisch-Egyptisch Genootschap, ex Oriente Lux, *Jaarbericht* No. 15 (1957-58).

has, no doubt for good reason, been translated as "sodomites" in the Old Testament.[81]

There is more evidence for such prostitution in the service of Ishtar in secular Roman literature. Both Lucian and Apuleius tell a similar story of a man turned into an ass by magic, and sold to a gang of rascally, effeminate and homosexual priests of Ishtar, who carry the goddess around the villages, perform rites of self-mutilation, collect offerings, and have sex with the occasional lusty villager when possible.

Philo of Alexandria venomously denounces such effeminate priests in pre-Christian Egypt (see below).

Early Christian sources also are clear about these prostitutes as they existed in historical times. Eusebius tells how his admired emperor Constantine destroyed a wicked temple at "Aphaca," where "men undeserving of the name forgot the dignity of their sex, and propitiated the demon [Ishtar] by their effeminate conduct."[82]

Gibbon confirms these actions of Constantine: "the effeminate priests of the Nile were abolished," he says, and he notes "the destruction of several temples in Phoenicia, in which every mode of prostitution was devoutly practiced in the face of day."[83]

Evidently the ruins may survive to the present day: the intrepid Victorian explorer, Sir Richard F. Burton, notes in his "Terminal Essay" to

---

81. Westermarck, Edward: *The History of Human Marriage* (New York, 1922), vol. i, p. 224.

82. Eusebius, *The Life of Constantine*, in *Select Library of the Nicene and Post-Nicene Fathers*, chap. 55 (Grand Rapids, 1952).

83. Gibbon, vol. ii, chap. 21, p. 415.

the *Arabian Nights* that the site (Aphaca) is now known as Wadi al-Afik, "on the route from Bayrut to the Cedars."

So, the nature of the *kedeshim* seems clear enough.

As a result, we can formulate the historical Jewish attitude towards male homosexuality with some exactness.

The Hebrew word *to'ebah* ("abomination") signifies something intrinsically evil, a religious sin, an idolatry. It is particularly associated with idolatrous worship and the Canaanites. Its connection with idolatry is patent even within the passages regarding homosexual acts, because religious homosexual acts were part of the Canaanite worship of Ishtar. The internal consistency is obvious in I Kings 14:24: "Worse still, all over the country there were male prostitutes attached to the shrines, and the people adopted all the abominable practices of the [Canaanites]." In this way, for the Jews, male homosexuality came to be a paradigm of *to'ebah*, the one abomination which every Jew must refrain from, under penalty of death.

The Messianic Tradition

The messianic tradition is one of the keys to the mythico-religious understanding of Jewish history—a trait which set them off from their neighbors as surely as the cultivation of pederasty distinguished the Greeks.

The primitive roots of this tradition are not unusual. The word "messiah" has the same root meaning as its Greek translation "Christ"—anointed. Anything receiving holy oil from the priest was *mashiach*: shields, swords, soldiers and so forth. If the priest anointed you, that made you *mashiach*. In this original sense of the term, Israel has had several messiahs: Saul and David were, among many others, legitimately anointed kings of Yahweh.

In its original usage, when Yahwism (early Judaism) was a war-cult, the messianic tradition implied military dominance of the earth by the anointed Jewish priest-king.[84]

---

84. Riggan, George A.: *Messianic Theology and Christian Faith*, p. 11 (Philadelphia, 1978).

The Jews did not originally have kings, being a pastoral and nomadic folk who ruled themselves through decisions reached in the Tent of Meeting. This way of life was endangered by the surrounding military empires, which were highly centralized and dangerous. It is commonly supposed that the kings of Israel were a reflex institution, borrowed from the Canaanites and others, not original with the Jews.[85] Yahwism emerges from prehistory as a loose association of tribes for the perpetuation of a cult, the leading elements of that cult being ritual, oracle and holy war.[86]

Holy war involved taboos and ritual preparation, for the leadership of the hero (or messiah) was a "special gift manifesting the outpouring of Yahweh's spirit."[87]

The earliest tradition called the messianic generals "judges," probably because they decided all questions having to do with the will of Yahweh. They were momentarily "inspired" to do great deeds while anointed, but the "judgeship" was not hereditary; by nature it could not be: the judgeship did not even necessarily last an entire lifetime.

This institution was destroyed by the Philistines, who profited from its weakness (no continuity of policy was possible). During their war on the Jews, the Philistines stole the Ark of the Covenant, a loss which threatened the cultural identity of the Jews.

Probably in response to this catastrophe, the next judge, Samuel, began anointing genuine kings. The first anointed was Saul. When Saul died, Samuel anointed David. This action precipitated a civil war in

---

85. Riggan, p. 12.
86. Riggan, pp. 14-15.
87. Riggan, p. 16.

Israel: the north sided with Saul's heirs, while the south sided with the new king, David.

David was successful beyond anyone's expectations. Around 1,000 BC, he captured Jerusalem and began rapidly absorbing the traditions of the defeated Canaanite kings. Perceiving his success, the north abandoned the civil war and acclaimed David as *mashiach* of Israel and Judah. David proceeded to the conquest of Palestine and the recovery of the Ark of the Covenant.[88] In addition, David launched a new fashion and figure of speech in referring to the messiah, that is himself, the anointed king, as "the [firstborn] son of God."[89]

Along with this new terminology, David borrowed other traditions of Oriental rulers. One of his priests, Nathan, received a vision of a covenant between Yahweh and the *house of David*. This was written down as a new supplement to the original covenant between Yahweh and the Jewish people; the oldest text of this agreement bears a "striking resemblance to the Egyptian royal record."[90] We find this text in II Samuel 7:16, among other places:

> Your family shall be established and your kingdom shall stand for
> all time in my sight, and your throne shall be established forever.

---

88. Riggan, p. 19.
89. *Encyclopedia Britannica*: "Judaism, History of." Riggan, p. 25. Psalms 2:7.
90. Riggan, p. 22.

The Psalms of the Old Testament also show an extensive borrowing from Egyptian and Mesopotamian court literature. Since David was such a thorough Canaanizer, we may suppose that he did not abolish the temple prostitutes in the city of Jerusalem. (In any case, the record indicates that they were flourishing under his son, Solomon.) His well-known love affair with Jonathan would not seem to suggest that he was intolerant of same-sex behavior.

David's grandson, Rehoboam, had a troubled reign. The new Davidic regime demanded forced labor from the Jews, and this, along with general opposition to the Canaanite transformation of the Jewish state, caused the north to secede again. The newly divided Israel lapsed into a long period of religious reform and decay, where cult worship, purification of the faith, and scathing prophets came and went with regularity. There was a devastating attack from the Assyrians, followed by the uncompromising reign of Josiah, who reinstituted the Passover and attempted to destroy all the pagan temples.

> He [Josiah] suppressed the heathen priests whom the kings of Judah had appointed to burn sacrifices at the hill-shrines…as well as those who burnt sacrifices to Baal, to the sun and moon and planets and all the host of heaven. He took the symbol of Asherah from the house of the LORD…and pounded it to dust.…He also pulled down the houses of the male prostitutes attached to the house of the LORD, where the women wove vestments in honor of Asherah. He brought in all the priests from the cities of Judah and desecrated the hill-shrines where they had burnt sacrifices, from Geba to Beersheba, and dismantled the hill-shrines of the demons in front of the gate of Joshua…He desecrated Topeth in

the Valley of Ben-hinnom....He destroyed the horses that the kings of Judah had set up in honour of the sun....[91]

There was never such a severe priest-king as Josiah; at least such is the claim of the Old Testament.

Josiah's purification of the faith was not effective in the domain of practical politics. Harassed by Egypt, Babylon and Assyria, Israel finally succumbed to a series of Babylonian attacks beginning in 605 BC and culminating in 587. Babylonian forces obliterated the towns of Judah and destroyed both Jerusalem and its Temple. The Israeli king's sons were slain before his eyes; he was then blinded and taken off into exile with most of the remaining Jewish population. This was the end of messianic royalism as an effective political force among the Jews.[92]

What followed was largely a process of assuming guilt and assessing blame. The "Deuteronomist" placed the blame on the institution of the monarchy as "the fundamental act of unfaith toward Yahweh responsible for the Babylonian captivity."[93]

Whatever the reason, God had broken his purported covenants with the Jewish people and the house of David.

> I have sworn by my holiness once and for all,
> I will not break my word to David,

---

91. II Kings 23.
92. Riggan, p. 34.
93. Riggan, p. 21.

his posterity shall continue for ever,
his throne before me like the sun;
it shall be sure for ever as the moon's return,
faithful so long as the skies remain.

Yet thou [Yahweh] hast rejected thy anointed king,
thou hast spurned him and raged against him,
thou hast denounced the covenant with thy servant,
defiled his crown and flung it to the ground.
Thou hast breached his walls
and laid his fortresses in ruin;
all who pass by plunder him,
and he suffers the taunts of his neighbors.
Thou hast increased the power of his enemies
and brought joy to all his foes;
thou hast let his sharp sword be driven back
and left him without help in the battle.
Thou hast put an end to his glorious rule
and hurled his throne to the ground;
thou hast cut short the days of his youth and vigour
and covered him with shame.

How long, O Lord, wilt thou hide thyself from sight?[94]

---
94. Psalms 89: 35-46.

In the face of such a catastrophe, the people of Israel, for reasons now intrinsic to their culture, came to the conclusion that God had broken his covenant because they had incurred his anger. A corollary of this conclusion was that improving their conduct would bring about a return of what was already being perceived as the Golden Age of the Hebrews—that is, they would return to Israel with a messiah leading them just as David had.

This belief is what scholars usually call "the messianic tradition." It is a tradition of a *future* messiah, as opposed to the real and present messiahs we have been observing. Beginning with the Babylonian exile, the Jewish people began to wait for a new messiah, and there was to be no lack of claimants. The new emphasis on strict religious conduct coincided with the Jews' liberation under the violently anti-homosexual Persians, and the addition of the anti-homosexual prohibitions to the Holiness Books of Leviticus.

To conclude: the Jews developed from a pastoral, nomadic nation to a centralized kingship under external pressure, and experienced a catastrophic failure of that kingship in 587 BC. As a result of their earlier messianic tradition and the catastrophe, the Jews elaborated a belief in a future messiah who was destined to save all Israel (and set it to rule over the earth, as well). Faith in Yahweh had been present from the beginning, and was also to be elaborated into what finally became "faith in faith." On the most primitive level, this belief is magical: if things are going badly for you or the nation, it is because you lack faith. This philosophical tradition, which stands in stark contrast to that of the Greeks and the Romans, was to have a profound influence on Christianity.

Jew and Greek in Conflict

After the Babylonian exile had led to an increasing codification of Jewish laws (including, it would seem, the anti-homosexual provisions newly added to Leviticus), another quirk of historical chance brought the Jews into direct contact with the Greeks under the worst of circumstances: the Greeks of the Hellenistic period conquered Palestine in the second century BC.

Mutual acquaintance does not seem to have led to mutual esteem in this instance. It appears that the Jews and the Greeks developed a profound, mutual loathing and contempt. This is the testimony of the contemporary witnesses; the "culture shock" of the Jews was the deeper because they had, once again, been vanquished.

Brought into contact with a culture that not only tolerated pederasty but glorified it, the Jews reacted with disgust. It seems likely that the elaboration of the grand myth of Sodom dates from this time—"Sodom" would have served admirably as a code word to denote the despised Greek conquerors.

The Jewish hatred of Greeks and Greek culture has endured well into the present century—Chaim Potok has vivid memories of his own childhood:

> When I was young, the cultural specter I was taught to look upon with revulsion as I made my way painstakingly through labyrinthine passages of Talmud…was the Greece of Dionysus

and Aristotle. None of my teachers ever uttered the words used by the medieval Jewish thinker Nachmanides, who wrote of Aristotle, "May his name be erased." But similar words, spoken and unspoken, floated through the corridors of my school. Greece was the idolatrous menace we most despised and feared.[95]

Such surviving bitterness suggests that the initial encounter was not particularly amicable, and indeed it was not. Having rejected Ishtar and pulled down the houses of the *kedeshim*, having experienced the exile and the return, the Jews could not understand the Greeks as anything other than demons in human form. The Greeks, on their part, seem to have reacted with condescension, trying to order the life of the Jews in accordance with the lives of similar "barbarians" living in Palestine. An advisor to Antiochus IV (167 BC) prescribed a religious cult similar to that of the Phoenicians.

The result was, from the Jewish point of view, that "the abomination of desolation" (*i.e.* idols) were placed on the altar of the Temple of Jerusalem. The new religious practices were forced upon the Jews by their scientific Greek conquerors. Troops forced Jews to eat pork.

The Jews loathed their new religion and they loathed the Greeks. The idea of a gymnasium (where one trains in the nude) was abhorrent to them, as was the Greek idea of calisthenics (which means *beautiful strength*). They already knew, by now, that homosexual behavior was a

---

[95]. Potok, Chaim: *Wanderings* (paperback edition, New York, 1980).

paradigm of abomination (or *to'ebah*), and Greek culture was, for the moment, rejected entirely and out of hand. One gymnasium would be the cause of a twenty-five year war between the two cultures.

In turn, the Greeks seem not to have paid any attention to the Jewish religion, regarding it merely as a mass of scribal pollution of what must have been the Jews' true (barbarian) religion. It is not far off the mark to say that the two main contributors to western thought missed each other entirely on their first meeting: ships passed in the night.

It is also clear that many of the conflicts thrown into relief during this first encounter between the Jews and the Greeks are still present within what we now call the "Judæo-Christian tradition."

The work of attempting to reconcile the two traditions began on an informal basis almost immediately, as the Jews began reading the works of the Greeks. It was to continue at a rapid pace in the city of Alexandria during and after the life of Christ. For, as Potok remarked, the Jews not only detested the Greeks, they feared them as well. A primary tactic in dealing with a feared enemy is to master his books.

The World of Hellenism

To summarize the principal developments so far, it is clear that the two arguments most commonly deployed against homosexual behavior had already been formulated by this time, and were present as an intellectual undercurrent in parts of the Hellenistic world. The first, Jewish, argument, is simply that God hates homosexuals (and wants them dead). The second, Platonic, argument is that homosexuality violates the laws of nature.

The fact that both arguments are without merit has surely not prevented them from a long, baleful career. The first "argument" is not an argument at all, but an arbitrary assertion about the unknowable, which can only be countered with an equally arbitrary counter-assertion. (The Reverend Troy Perry has done it: "God loves homosexuals.") The second argument is much more problematic, since it seems to be without meaning, just as surely as the word "nature" is without meaning.

The word is most commonly interpreted as "the great outdoors": here it seems to denote anything untouched by mankind, and by implication subsumes all of humanity and its doings into the category of "the unnatural." In this sense, a beaver-dam is a natural phenomenon and a sidewalk is not, although both are artificial constructions by animals. The antihumanist implications of such a definition of "nature" are intriguing, but irrelevant to the present argument. If humanity and its works are "unnatural," then there is no evidence that homosexual behavior can, under this rationale, be singled out from the rest of human activity.

Of course, in another sense, "nature" simply denotes the entire universe, which obeys certain known laws of operation—the laws of gravitation and so on. The key here is that it is *not possible to violate the laws of nature*. Mechanical flight, for example, long regarded as highly unnatural, has extended man's knowledge of natural laws; it has not violated them. (The same may prove to be true of homosexual behavior, when scholars of the future undertake a serious and impartial study of the phenomenon.)

In a third sense, the term "nature" is simply seized as a "word of power" to apply to whatever the speaker admires or likes. When used in such a fashion, "nature" has no meaning at all.

In any case, all that was needed at this point in time was a new synthesis of these two homophobic arguments, and this was to be provided by the Christian religion, especially as it was elaborated in its most ancient home, the Mediterranean city of Alexandria.

Alexandria had been, already for some centuries, a home to a large number of the Jews of the Diaspora—Jews who were no longer fluent in Hebrew, having adopted Greek as their daily tongue. Much of the intertestamental, or apocryphal, literature was written in Alexandria, and it was written by Greek-speaking Jews. The book of *II Maccabees*, for example, although written in Greek, charges its enemies (Jewish back-sliders) with two concrete crimes: Greek calisthenics (which were conducted in the nude) and the wearing of Greek hats. The Old Testament had been translated into Greek so that the Hellenizing Jews could read their scriptures (the Greek version is known as the Septuagint). The great library of Alexandria contained almost 700,000 rolls of manuscript, most of them in Greek.

Since the Jews of Alexandria only knew the Old Testament in Greek, the new intertestamental literature produced in Alexandria and elsewhere was indistinguishable from the "real thing." These books were, somewhat uncritically, read and revered by the early Christians, and were often cited as sacred scripture. St. Jerome discovered the error when preparing his Latin Vulgate.

The error is perhaps instructive as an example of the ultra-Platonic mind-cast at its worst: the religious elders claim to be divinely inspired, and to be holding the word of God in their hands; a few centuries pass and a discovery is made that books A, B and C were, after all, *not* the word of God. No apology is offered; the priesthood continues as before, discarding the works previously held as sacred. To openly admit that one had made an error in defining the body of Scripture would lead to too many questions.

As a whole, the production of the Hellenizing Jews is held by most critics and scholars to be of fairly poor quality. *IV Maccabees*, supposedly a book of the Old Testament, was a plagiarism of Plato's *Gorgias*,[96] and the Jew who borrowed extensively from Plato to compose his book of wisdom unblushingly called it *The Wisdom of Solomon*—another untruth deployed in the service of the "true religion."

The Greeks had an enormous influence on the Jews during the Hellenistic era. Many analysts summarize the period by saying that the influence only went in one direction—the Old Testament went into Greek, the Jews were writing and speaking Greek, and so forth. But our history does not end here, in the twilight of Hellenism. In later years, Jewish teachings were to have a profound influence on western culture.

It may be noted that the Hellenizing Jews and the Platonists were not the only inhabitants of Alexandria. The city teemed with every religious and philosophical influence; science was making good progress among

---

96. Hadas, Moses: *Hellenistic Culture*, p. 79 (New York, 1959).

those of the Aristotelian mind-cast; mystery religions flourished. Mankind was entering an age of anxiety, as the old complex of pagan beliefs was confused by the bright light of skepticism. Charlatans and fortune-tellers abounded. People sought prosperity and truth in many different ways, and it must not be imagined that the Græco-Roman tradition of pederasty was falling into neglect; on the contrary, the Hellenistic world saw a flowering of verse in celebration of the love of boys—verse which has miraculously survived in the pages of *The Greek Anthology*.

*

Love has found out how to mix
Beauty with beauty. Not
Emerald with gold, which does not
Gleam and sparkle like these do,
Nor ivory with ebony,
Less dark and light than these are,
But Kleandros and Eubotis—
Flowers of Love and Persuasion.[97]

*

Zephyr, kindliest of winds,
Fetch back my loved one, Euphragoras,
Extend not that sojourn you began:
Brief months stretch to years for us in love.[98]

---

97. These selections are from *The Greek Anthology*, either the Loeb or the Penguin edition. The Loeb is Volume 4 of the Anthology, Book 12 (Strato's *Muse of Boy Love*). This one is Asklepiades, 12.163: Penguin p. 62, trans. Rexroth.

98. Dioskorides, 12.171: Penguin p. 115, trans. Whigham.

*

As honey in wine / wine, honey
Alexis in Cleobulus
Cleobulus in Alexis
sweet-haired & lovely each
as he with whom the other
mingles…product
of such two entwined
potent
as vineyards of deathless Cypris.[99]

*

I am caught,
I who once laughed often
at the serenades of young men crossed in
love.
And at thy gate,
Myiscus,
Winged Eros has fixed me,
Inscribing on me
"Spoils won from Chastity."[100]

*

Delicate children, so help me Love,
doth Tyre nurture,

---

99. Meleager, 12.164: Penguin pp. 142-3, trans. Whigham.
100. Meleager, 12.23: Loeb p. 293, trans. Paton.

> But Myiscus is the sun that,
> when his light bursts forth,
> quenches the stars.[101]

*

> The breath of life—no less,
> this rope that constrains
> me, Myiscus, to you
> —you have me fast.

> Sweet boy,
> even a deaf-mute
> could *hear* what you *look*!
> Look blackly at me,
> winter breaks out in clouds.
> Smile with clear eyes,
> & spring giggles
> coating me with petals.[102]

*

> Boy, hold my wreath for me.
> The night is black,
> the path is long,
> And I am completely and beautifully drunk.
> Nevertheless I will go

---

101. Meleager, 12.59: Loeb p. 311, trans. Paton.
102. Meleager, 12.159: Penguin p. 145, trans. Whigham.

to Themison's house and sing beneath his window.
You need not come with me:
though I may stumble,
He is a steady lamp for the feet of love.[103]

*

Yesterday I dined with Demetrius, the boys'
gymnastics teacher, luckiest of men. One was lying
in his lap, one was draped on his shoulder,
one served him
food, one drink—what a quartet!
So I said to him (in jest)
"Good friend, do you
have exercises for them at night, too?"[104]

*

I delight in the prime of a boy twelve,
But a thirteen-year-old's better yet.

At fourteen he's Love's even sweeter flower,
And one going on fifteen's even more delightful.

Sixteen belongs to the gods, and seventeen…
It's not for me, but for Zeus to seek.

---

103. Anonymous, 12.116: Penguin p. 162, trans. Fitts.
104. Automedon, 12.34: Penguin p. 229, trans. Merwin.

The World of Hellenism • 85

> If you want the older ones, you don't play
> any more, but seek *& answer back*.[105]
>
> *
>
> Long hair, endless curls trained by the devoted
> "Artistry" of a stylist beyond the call of
> Nature, do nothing for me. What I like's a
> boy's body hot from the park, all grimy
> And the sight of his flesh rubbed down with oil.
> Nice, and artless; none of the pretty "enchantment"
> Laid on by your merchants of the romantic.[106]

Finally, it may be useful to include a piece of raw primary data which is still being assimilated by scholarship, in the hope that it may aid our inquiry on two fronts. First, it gives us some idea of the sort of nonsense one was likely to come across in contemporary Alexandria. Second, it would seem to be evidence that the elaboration of the grand myth of Sodom by the early Christian church as a paradigm of human evil was not an endeavor which met with universal agreement.

The following citations are from the writings of the Gnostics, a term which covers a great variety of early versions of the Christian faith, all of which were suppressed by the later Catholic faith. As would become their too-frequent habit, the triumphant Catholics burned the books of the defeated enemy, and thus the books of the Gnostics perished. By a great

---

105. Strato, 12.4: Penguin p. 271, trans. Meyer.
106. Strato, 12.192: Penguin p. 273, trans. Hogge.

chance, however, some of them have survived to the present day: they were evidently buried outside a Gnostic monastery in Egypt before the great Catholic purge and burning, and lay unknown and untouched in a clay jar until December, 1945. After their discovery and a struggle for their ownership, they finally became available in a rough translation in 1977. Here are some of the things preached by some of the Gnostic Christians:

> Then there came forth from that place the great power of the great light Plesithea, the mother of the angels, the mother of the lights, the glorious mother, the virgin with the four breasts, bringing the fruit from Gomorrah as spring and Sodom, which is the fruit of the spring of Gomorrah which is in her. She came forth through the great Seth.[107]

> Then the great angel Hormos came to prepare, through the virgins of the corrupted sowing of this Aeon, in a Logos-begotten, holy vessel, through the Holy Spirit, the seed of the great Seth.

> Then the great Seth came and brought his seed. And it was sown in the Aeons which had been brought forth, their number being the amount of Sodom. Some say that Sodom is the place of pasture of the great Seth, which is Gomorrah. But others say that the great Seth took his plant out of Gomorrah and planted it in the second place to which he gave the name Sodom.

---

107. *The Gospel of the Egyptians*, III, 2, 56, trans. Bohlig and Wisse in Robinson, James M.: *The Nag Hammadi Library*, p. 201 (New York, 1981).

This is the race which came forth through Edokla. For she gave birth through the word to Truth and Justice, the origin of the seed of eternal life which is with those who will persevere because of the knowledge of their emanation. This is the great, incorruptible race which has come forth through three worlds to the world.[108]

When he will have appeared, O Shem, upon the earth, in the place which shall be called Sodom, then safeguard the insight which I shall give you. For those whose heart was pure will congregate to you, because of the word which you will reveal. For when you appear in the world, dark Nature will shake against you, together with the winds and a demon, that they may destroy the insight. But you, proclaim quickly to the Sodomites your universal teaching, for they are your members. For the demon of human form will part from that place by my will, since he is ignorant. He will guard this utterance. But the Sodomites, according to the will of the Majesty, will bear witness to the universal testimony. They will rest with a pure conscience in the place of their repose, which is the unbegotten Spirit. And as these things will happen, Sodom will be burned unjustly by a base nature. For the evil will not cease in order that your majesty may reveal that place.[109]

---

108. *Ibid.*, III, 2, 60, p. 202.
109. *The Paraphrase of Shem*, VII, 1, 29 in Robinson, p. 321.

PHILO OF ALEXANDRIA

Philo of Alexandria (c. 20 BC-50 AD) is a little-known philosopher (except among specialists). He invites attention because of his central role in the foundation of Christian dogma and philosophy; he probably had as much influence on the early church fathers as St. Paul, or Christ himself. Certainly Philo was the principal bridge between Platonic philosophy and Christian theology. Professor Wolfson, a noted Philomaniac, has even shown that such elements of the patristic philosophy as the Trinity and the Incarnation—unknown to Philo—are nevertheless constructed on the foundation established by Philo.[110]

Philo's enormous influence on Christian doctrine is slightly unusual because he was not a Christian, but a Jew residing in Alexandria, and a part of that Greek-speaking Jewish tradition which gave birth to the early Christian church. He was also a leader of the attempts to synthesize the Greek and Jewish traditions.

---

110. Hadas, *Hellenistic Culture*, p. 77. See also Gibbon, vol. 2, chapter 21, pp. 355-9.

Philo's belief in the possibility of harmonizing Plato and the Old Testament is in itself a symptom of his Platonic, *a priori* thinking. The two pre-eminent compilations of ancient wisdom must, according to this view, amount to the same thing, since the Forms are the same in all times for all men. By contrast, an Aristotelian approach to the subject would weigh and evaluate both sources in their cultural context, and then dispassionately note similarities and differences, advancing cautiously to general statements.

Philo's work can be characterized as the first great Christian exegesis—exegesis being the critical analysis and explanation of important texts, particularly religious ones. Philo produced a detailed and implausible exegesis of the Pentateuch, an effort to make the laws of Moses conform to the wisdom of Plato. In the process, he corrupted both. As Moses Hadas points out:

> Philo's adaptations of Plato may force the meaning of Plato unduly (but not nearly so much as he forces the meaning of Scripture) yet he never takes open issue with Plato, as he does with the Stoics, and is plainly unaware that he may be doing violence to Plato. The nature of his Platonism may be illustrated by a single instance: the Scriptural passage which speaks of God creating man "in the image of God" he declares must apply to the whole of the visible world.[111]

---

111. Hadas, p. 76.

Graeco-Roman thinking about male homoeroticism has already been presented in this book, as well as the attitudes of the Old Testament. It is interesting and instructive to note the efforts of a man who believed he was putting the two traditions together. His Jewish culture and religion probably assured the triumph of the negative, but whatever the cause of it, Philo's negativism was to have a profound influence on the thinking of the fathers of the Church.

In the first passage offered for inspection, Philo undertakes to inform the reader about the two *Symposia* of Xenophon and Plato:

> Xenophon's banquet is closer to common humanity. There are flute girls, dancers, jugglers, fun-makers, proud of their ability for jesting and being witty, and other features inducing yet greater cheer and relaxation.

> Plato's banquet is almost entirely concerned with love, not merely with men madly in love with women [sic], or women with men, but of men for males differing from them only in age. For even if there is some contrived subtlety concerning Eros and Heavenly Aphrodite, it is brought in by way of jest. The greater part is taken up with common and vulgar love, which not only robs men of courage, the virtue most useful for life in peace as well as war, but produces in their souls the disease of effeminacy and renders androgynous those who should have been trained in all the pursuits making for valor. And having ruined their years of boyhood, and degraded them to the class and condition of sex objects [trans. sic], it injures the lovers, too, in the most essential respects, body, mind, and property. For the mind of the boy-lover is necessarily aimed at his darling, and is keen-sighted for him only, blind to all other interests, private and public; his body wastes away through lust, especially if he fail in his suit, while his property is diminished from either

end by his neglecting it and expending it on his beloved. As a side-effect there is another still greater evil touching everyone, for they artificially contrive the desolation of cities, the scarcity of the best sorts of men, and barrenness and sterility, by imitating those ignorant of the science of husbandry, sowing not in the deep soil of the plain but in briny fields and stony-hard places, which are not only of such a nature as to allow nothing to grow, but even destroy the seed planted in them.[112]

Now here, *pace* Hadas, Philo clearly takes open issue with Plato, and also does violence to him. Anyone who has read Plato's *Symposium* will notice that Philo's report of it contains not one thought which is recognizably derived from that dialogue. The mention of Plato's work is a mere pretext for a tirade against homosexual behavior in general, and pederasty in particular.

No one in Alexandria seems to have attempted the synthesis of Greek and Jewish thought by adapting the philosophy of Aristotle. In every case, the Greek of choice was Plato. Perhaps Aristotle simply could not be forced into the role—witness Philo's attitude towards science and the rational investigation of the universe.

Philo generally holds that man should put absolute trust in God and ignore the feeble efforts of reason. In this attitude, he is just as severe as our modern Christian Scientists:

---

112. Philo: *The Contemplative Life* in *Philo of Alexandria*, trans. David Winston (Paulist Press, Ramsey N.J., 1981).

> It is best then to trust in God and not in obscure reasonings and insecure conjectures....But if we mistakenly trust our private reasonings we shall construct and build the city of the mind that destroys the truth....For to trust God is a true teaching, but to trust empty reasonings is a lie....For it is truly irrational to put trust in plausible reasonings.[113]

Philo mentions in passing the benefits to be derived from this ultra-Platonic philosophy: "so that, having already once had a share of unerring opinion, he might exchange unreliable doubt for an absolutely firm conviction."[114]

Doctors are not to be trusted: "This is an attribute of virtually all those who vacillate, even though they do not concede it in so many words. When anything befalls them that does not accord with their wish, inasmuch as they do not maintain a firm trust in God their Savior, they flee first to creaturely aid, to physicians, herbs, drug compounds, a strict regimen, and all the other aids employed by mortals. And if one say to them, 'Flee, foolish ones, to the one and only physician of soul disorders and abandon the falsely designated help of created being, subject to suffering,' they laugh and mock..."[115]

---

113. Philo: *Legum Allegorarium* 3.228-9 in Winston, pp. 150-1.
114. Philo: *De Posteritate Caini* 13, in Winston p. 151.
115. Philo: *De Sacrificiis Abelis et Caini* 70-71, in Winston p. 152.

What then of schools and education? "But when God brings forth young shoots of self-taught wisdom in the soul, we must immediately terminate and destroy the knowledge that comes from teaching....God's pupil...can no longer suffer the guidance of men."[116]

While the twentieth-century mind may find such thinking bizarre, it is important to realize that such teachings were to have a long influence on later intellectual history.

It remains to discover what Philo thinks about homosexuality. His attitude has been sampled above, but Philo has not yet been presented in full cry. The following citations are repugnant, but are transcribed in full simply because so many people do not have easy access to Philo. While they do not make pleasant reading, they are a key to later Christian teaching on the subject.

> The land of the Sodomites, a part of the land of Canaan afterwards called Palestinian Syria, was brimful of innumerable iniquities, particularly such as arise from gluttony and lewdness, and multiplied and enlarged every other possible pleasure with so formidable a menace that it had at last been condemned by the Judge of All. The inhabitants owed this extreme licence to the never-failing lavishness of their sources of wealth, for deep-soiled and well-watered as it was, the land

---

116. *Ibid.*, 78-9, in Winston p. 206.

had every year a prolific harvest of all manner of fruits, and the chief beginning of evils, as one has aptly said, is goods in excess. Incapable of bearing such satiety, plunging like cattle, they threw off from their necks the law of nature and applied themselves to deep drinking of strong liquor and dainty feeding and forbidden forms of intercourse. Not only in their mad lust for women did they violate the marriages of their neighbours, but also men mounted males without respect for the sex nature which the active partner shares with the passive; and so when they tried to beget children they were discovered to be incapable of any but a sterile seed. Yet the discovery availed them not, so much stronger was the force of the lust which mastered them. Then, as little by little they accustomed those who were by nature men to submit to playing the part of women, they saddled them with the formidable curse of a female disease. For not only did they emasculate their bodies by luxury and voluptuousness but they worked a further degeneration in their whole soul and, as far as in them lay, were corrupting the whole of mankind. Certainly, had Greeks and barbarians then joined together in affecting such unions, city after city would have become a desert, as though depopulated by a pestilential sickness.

But God, moved by pity for mankind whose Saviour and Lover he was, gave increase in the greatest possible degree to the unions which men and women naturally make for the begetting of children, but abominated and extinguished this unnatural and forbidden intercourse, and those who lusted for such He cast forth and chastised with punishments not of the usual kind but startling and extraordinary, newly-created for this purpose. He bade the air grow suddenly overcrowded and pour forth a great rain, not of water but fire. And when the flames streamed down massed in one constant and perpetual rush, they burnt up the fields and the meadows, the leafy groves, the overgrowths of the marshlands and the dense thickets....And when the flame had utterly consumed all that was visible and above ground it penetrated right down into the earth itself, destroyed its inherent life-power and reduced it to complete sterility to prevent it from ever bearing fruit and herbage at all. And to this day it goes on burning, for the fire of the thunderbolt is never quenched, but either continues its ravages or else smoulders. And the clearest proof of that is still visible, for a monument of the disastrous event remains in the smoke which rises ceaselessly and the brimstone which the miners obtain, while the ancient prosperity of the country is most plainly attributed by the survival of one of the cities of the neighbourhood and the land around it; for the city is thickly populated and the land rich in corn and pasturage and fertile in general, thus providing a standing evidence to the sentence decreed by the divine judgement.[117]

And here is the first attempt at synthesis—Philo has combined the Jewish and Platonic arguments against homosexual behavior ("forbidden by God" and "against nature," respectively) and woven them into a fanatically homophobic tapestry unique to the early Christian church, a

---

117. Philo: *On Abraham* 133-41 in *Philo*, Volume VI, trans. F. H. Colson, pp. 69-73 (Loeb Library, Cambridge, 1959).

background which is, it would seem, well-prepared to give birth to that most Christian of all words, "sodomy."

While many may find the tirade above distasteful, there is worse to be found, in another work of Philo's.

> Much graver than the above is another evil which has ramped its way into the cities, namely pederasty. In former days the very mention of it was a great disgrace, but now it is a matter of boasting not only to the active but to the passive partners, who habituate themselves to endure the disease of effemination, let both body and soul run to waste, and leave no ember of their male sex-nature to smoulder. Mark how conspicuously they braid and adorn the hair of their heads, and how they scrub and paint their faces with cosmetics and pigments and the like, and smother themselves with fragrant unguents. For of all such embellishments, used by all who deck themselves out to wear a comely appearance, fragrance is the most seductive. In fact the transformation of the male nature is practised by them as an art and does not raise a blush. These persons are rightly judged worthy of death by those who obey the law, which ordains that the man-woman who debases the sterling coin of nature should perish unavenged, suffered not to live for a day or even an hour, as a disgrace to himself, his house, his native land and the whole human race. And the lover of such may be assured that he is subject to the same penalty. He pursues an unnatural pleasure and does his best to render cities desolate and uninhabited by destroying the means of procreation. Furthermore he sees no harm in becoming a tutor and instructor in the grievous vices of unmanliness and effeminacy by prolonging the bloom of the young and emasculating the flower of their prime, which should rightly be trained to strength and robustness. Finally, like a bad husbandman he lets the deep-soiled and fruitful beds lie sterile,

by taking steps to keep them from bearing, while he spends his labour night and day on soil from which no growth at all can be expected. The reason is, I think, to be found in the prizes awarded in many nations to licentiousness and effeminacy. Certainly you may see these hybrids of men and women continually strutting about through the thick of the market, heading the processions at the feasts, appointed to serve as unholy ministers of unholy things, leading the mysteries and initiations and celebrating the rites of Demeter. Those of them who by way of heightening still further their youthful beauty have desired to be changed completely into women and gone on to mutilate their genital organs, are clad in purple like signal benefactors of their native lands, and march in front escorted by a bodyguard, attracting the attention of those who meet them. But if such indignation as our lawgiver felt was directed against those who do not shrink from such conduct, if they were cut off without condonation as public enemies, each of them a curse and pollution of his country, many others would be found to take warning. For relentless punishment of criminals already condemned acts as a considerable check on those who are eager to practise the like.[118]

---

118. Philo, *The Special Laws* 37-42 in the Loeb Philo, VII, pp. 499-501.

As John Lauritsen has pointed out, Boswell relegates all mention of this extremely homophobic philosopher to less-than-candid footnotes such as this one: "In his *De legibus specialibus* Philo contrasts Mosaic prohibitions of homosexual acts with their complete acceptance by Hellenistic society"—a summary of the passage above, believe it or not—and one would scarcely dream that Philo considered homosexuals so evil that they required instant execution by lynch law.[119]

Philo synthesized the Jewish and Greek homophobic arguments (although curiously ignoring Aristotle), and added enormously to the bitterness of what was there for his taking. He corrupted both his Jewish and his Greek sources without flinching, condemned reason and the sciences, and had almost no respect at all for any truth which was not one of his own *obiter dicta*. He lived and died about the same time as another Christian figure who now commands our attention.

---

119. Lauritsen, John: "*Culpa Ecclesiae*: Boswell's Dilemma" in *Homosexuality, Intolerance, and Christianity* (Gay Academic Union, New York, 1981).

Jesus

This charismatic faith-healer believed that a new era was at hand, and taught and acted accordingly. The new era—that is, the arrival of the Kingdom of God—is still awaited by modern Christians, but not as imminently as it appears to have been by Jesus himself. The following passage from Mark is echoed in many other places in the New Testament, and was one of the most important pillars of the new faith:

> Be watchful; I have foretold all to you. [Jesus now describes the end of the world.] But in those days after that affliction, the sun will be darkened, and the moon will not give her light, and the stars will be falling out of the sky, and the powers in the skies will be shaken. And then they will see the son of man coming in the clouds with great power and glory; and then he will send out his angels and gather his chosen together from the four winds, from the end of the earth to the end of the sky. [Now he predicts the date.] From the fig tree learn its parable. When its branch is tender and puts forth leaves, you know that the summer is near; so also you, when you see these things happening, know that he is near, at your doors. Truly, I

tell you that this generation will not pass by before all these things are done.[120]

The language, although metaphorical, is clear: the world will come to an end within the current generation. Albert Schweitzer contends that Jesus predicted these events within the current year.[121] Since this seems to have been an event which did not come to pass, it eventually became a problem for the new faith, and is traditionally referred to as the problem of the delayed *parousia*, the last word denoting the arrival of the kingdom of God.

This remarkable belief in the early arrival of the kingdom of God was central to Jesus' teaching and the teachings of the early Christian church. It is only within such a context that it makes any sense at all to preach universal chastity, or the other more extreme teachings of the gospels: if God is going to arrive in judgment at any moment, then one must strive for complete purity in every respect, and there is no need to worry about propagating the human species.

A second thread of importance in Jesus' teaching was faith-healing: like the belief in the rapid arrival of the kingdom of God, it was a central part of the belief system of the early church, and gradually receded in importance with the passage of time. When Jesus rose from the dead and gave his final instructions to the twelve apostles, he included the following exhortation:

---

120. Mark 13:30-32 (trans. Lattimore). Compare also Matthew 10:23, Mark 9:1, Matthew 24:34, and Luke 21:32.

121. Schweitzer, Albert: *The Quest of the Historical Jesus*, p. 358 (New York, 1961).

Go out into the world and preach the gospel to all creation. He who believes and is baptized shall be saved, but he who does not believe shall be condemned. And here are the signs that will go with the believers: In my name they will cast out demons, speak with tongues, hold snakes, and if they drink something lethal it cannot harm them, and they will lay their hands on the sick and these will be well.[122]

The many Christian debates over the details of dogma (well exemplified by the struggle between the *Homoousians* and the *Homoiousians*[123]) were fought with great vigor—indeed, with bloodshed—because the parties to the debates felt that the quality of dogma would directly influence the quality of belief. The quality of belief, in turn, influenced the ability to work miracles, as Christ himself had pointed out. The miracle-working, in turn, was the basis of the whole belief-structure, particularly in the days of the early church. An ability to cure the sick was not to be laughed at in those dismal, ignorant days, long before penicillin. Faith-healing still prospers in our own day; it is hard to imagine how attractive it was when medicine itself was another pseudo-science, no more respectable than alchemy or phrenology.

---

122. Mark 16.
123. The Homoousians thought that God the Father was of the same substance as Jesus Christ the Son, while the Homoiousians thought that the substance was only similar, not identical.

Although the passage of time has brought these doctrines into disfavor, it would be an anachronism to overlook their importance to the early church and to Jesus.

* * * * *

It would seem to be almost impossible to discover the opinions of Jesus regarding homosexuality—especially when eminent scholars sometimes hold that the search for the historical person is problematic. There are two clues in his cultural heritage and his single use of the word "faggot."[124] More tantalizing clues lie in his evident role as an outsider in his own society, his continuous association with the twelve male disciples, the lack of any reported marriage, his conspicuous consumption of wine, and his peculiar habit of initiating young men into "the mysteries of the Kingdom of God"—a rite which seemed to take all night and involve a modicum of clothing.

This last ritual is glimpsed in a recently discovered fragment of the gospel of Mark. In a letter to Theodore, Clement of Alexandria cited this gospel directly, while also stating that it was "secret" (which would seem to indicate that the early Christian church as he knew it was divided into exoteric and esoteric groups.)

In this letter, Clement makes the following claims:

---

124. Matthew 5:22, as explicated by Johansson, Warren: "Racha" in the *Encyclopedia of Homosexuality*, pp. 1093-1094 (New York, 1990).

…the secret Gospel brings in the following material word for word: "And they came into Bethany. And a certain woman whose brother had died was there. And, coming, she prostrated herself before Jesus and says to him, 'Son of David, have mercy upon me.' But the disciples rebuked her. And Jesus, being angered, went off with her into the garden where the tomb was, and straightway a great cry was heard from the tomb. And going near Jesus rolled away the stone from the door of the tomb. And straightway, going in where the youth was, he stretched forth his hand and raised him, seizing his hand. But the youth, looking upon him, loved him and began to beseech him that he might be with him. And going out of the tomb they came into the house of the youth, for he was rich. And after six days Jesus told him what to do and in the evening the youth comes to him, wearing a linen cloth over his naked body. And he remained with him that night, for Jesus taught him the mystery of the kingdom of God. And thence, arising, he returned to the other side of the Jordan."

After these words follows the text, "And James and John come to him," and all that section. But "naked man with naked man," and the other things about which you wrote, are not found.[125]

---

125. Smith, Morton: *Clement of Alexandria and a Secret Gospel of Mark* (Harvard University Press, 1973). A more popular version from the same author is *The Secret Gospel* (New York, 1973; Clearlake, California: 1982). The same author's *Jesus the Magician* is one of the best general overviews, along with Geza Vermes' *Jesus the Jew* and Michael Grant's *Jesus*. An excellent summary of the problems presented by the gospels and Christian mythmaking is Marcello Craveri's *The Life of Jesus.*

Since Clement claims to be citing the gospel of Mark, and since the text presents such an odd perspective on the earthly ministry of Jesus, we are bound to wonder if it is genuine. Its discoverer, Morton Smith, reviewed critical opinion ten years after reporting his find,[126] and reported that such opinion accepted the letter as a document produced by Clement of Alexandria, but was divided on the accuracy of Clement's attribution.

Smith himself feels that the secret fragment is stylistically so close to canonical Mark that a forgery is out of the question, but caution is still necessary in this murky area. It would be unwise to assume that this document has evidentiary value about Jesus without weighing a number of other factors—the Carpocratians may have possessed a gospel depicting Jesus in homosexual relations, but this tells us much more about the Carpocratians than about Jesus. Similarly, Clement's "secret gospel" is suspiciously gnostic in tone, implying that some sort of secret knowledge is necessary in order to enter the inner circle of the Christian church, but Christianity has never been a gnostic religion, and the Mar Saba manuscript probably tells us more about Clement and his circle than it tells us about Jesus.

A last clue to Jesus' views on homosexuality is the episode of the centurion's slave boy, healed by Jesus. This has been thoroughly reviewed by Donald Mader, who builds a persuasive case that the episode, if truly reported, shows that Jesus was far from homophobic.[127] Mader argues that the relationship between the centurion and his page boy was probably

---

126. Smith, Morton: "Clement of Alexandria and Secret Mark: The Score at the End of the First Decade," *Harvard Theological Review* 75:4 (1982), pp. 449-61.

127. Mader, Donald: "The *Entimos Pais* of Matthew 8:5-13 and Luke 7:1-10," *Paidika*, vol. 1, 1987, p. 27.

erotic—such relationships were well-known in Roman times—and that Jesus must have realized that the two men were lovers and bed-mates. Rather than use the occasion to deliver a sermon against the sins of Sodom, Jesus healed the slave boy without even mentioning the subject.

When all these clues are examined—even if they lead one to believe that Jesus was tolerant of homosexuality (or even, the unthinkable, a homosexual himself)—it must be remembered that the teachings of Jesus were to have surprisingly little influence on the development of Christian theology and doctrine. In the early years of the church, some of his principles were of central importance, but they gradually yielded to the doctrines developed by generations of theologians and doctors of the church. The issue of homoeroticism is an example: Jesus apparently never mentioned it, but St. Paul and many others did, and over the years an intense hatred of this phenomenon became central to Christianity.

It was bad luck for homosexual men that the Persian superstition was adopted by the Jews after the Babylonian exile; it was even worse luck that the elaboration and justification of the Christian hatred of homophilia was at its zenith at precisely the moment when Western civilization began its physical and intellectual conquest of the rest of the globe. The vast empires of the French and the British, and the later hegemony of America, brought the teachings of Western science to all the countries of the world—accompanied by a deadly and irrational homophobia rooted in their common religion.

St. Paul

St. Paul, in his early life known as Saul of Tarsus, was a contemporary of Philo and, like Philo, a Hellenized Jew.

It is somewhat surprising to realize that Paul's writings are the earliest extant Christian texts—earlier than any of the four gospels—and that these highly respected words were produced by a man who had never seen the Messiah he proclaimed to the world. Many, indeed, see Paul as the true founder of the Christian religion, whose indefatigable preaching to the Gentiles gave the new faith its strategic early mass.

Two doctrines make Paul's teachings particularly notable to historians of the early church—his reaffirmation of Jesus' doctrine of *salvation by faith*,[128] and his elaboration of the doctrine that *all sex is evil.*

The second teaching stemmed from a strong sensation of the inherent wickedness of the body itself. Paul considered *all* sexual acts to be inherently sinful, or Satanic. A saying attributed to Jesus echoes the common ground which lay between Paul and Jesus:

---

128. Galatians 3:1-6, 23-25.

> He said to them: Not all can accept this saying, but those to whom it is given. For there are sexless men who have been so from their mother's womb, and there are sexless men who have been made sexless by other men, and there are sexless men who have made themselves sexless for the sake of the Kingdom of Heaven. Let him who can accept, accept.[129]

This cryptic saying has a long and controversial history, centering on what it could possibly mean to "make oneself sexless for the sake of the Kingdom of Heaven." While the saying is probably a simple commendation of chastity, the apparent reference to eunuchs can give rise to another interpretation—that serious believers might want to voluntarily castrate themselves. The saying, which was accepted in its more disturbing sense by the early church father Origen[130]—is closely related to Jesus' central message, which was (and is) that the Kingdom of God is coming right away:[131] as a result, exceptional regulations are in effect. It is the same with Paul: the world is coming to an end, so we must give up every thought but that of eternal life.

> What I mean, my friends, is this. The time we live in will not last long. While it lasts, married men should be as if they had no wives; mourners should be as though they had nothing to grieve them, the joyful as if they did not rejoice; buyers must not count on keeping

---

129. Matthew 19:12.
130. Barnes, Timothy B.: *Constantine and Eusebius*, p. 83 (Cambridge, 1981).
131. Grant, Michael: *Jesus*—or, of course, the gospels themselves.

what they buy, nor those who use the world's wealth on using it to the full. For the whole frame of this world is falling away.[132]

As a result of the haste engendered by the imminent arrival of the end of the world, Paul was much more strict than any other teacher of sexual morality. All sex is perceived as part of the lower self, and therefore evil. "But if a man...has decided in his own mind to preserve his partner in her virginity, he will do well. Thus, he who marries his partner does well, and he who does not will do better."[133] It is interesting to note that this teaching, strictly interpreted, directly implies the extinction of the human race—a nefarious goal which the church fathers examined in this book habitually attributed to homosexual men.

Such a stringent suppression of the sexual drive is not held, by modern psychologists, to be "healthy." Many modern Christian marriage counselors tend to hold sacred the sexual act between husband and wife, as the "deepest expression of matrimonial love," or words to that effect. They have obviously abandoned the earliest Christian texts as irrelevant and possibly injurious; popular wisdom has it that the complete suppression of the libido is injurious to "mental health." Certainly, Paul's own meditations on the subject may give one pause:

> We know that the law is spiritual, but I am not: I am unspiritual, the purchased slave of sin. I do not even acknowledge my own

---

132. I Corinthians 7:29.
133. I Corinthians 7:37.

actions as mine, for what I do is not what I want to do, but what I detest. But if what I do is against my will, it means that I agree with the law, and hold it to be admirable. But as things are, it is no longer I who perform the action, but sin that lodges in me. For I know that nothing good lodges in me—in my unspiritual nature, I mean—for though the will to do good is there, the deed is not. The good which I want to do, I fail to do; but what I do is the wrong which is against my will; and if what I do is against my will, clearly it is no longer I who am the agent, but sin that has its lodging in me.[134]

When paired with the doctrine of justification by faith, this sort of teaching represents a marked decline in the Western philosophical tradition. Somehow, in its incoherent way, it manages to make the point that a Christian murderer is, in some important sense, "better" than a Jewish or pagan murderer, that evil done by Christians shall not be counted against them. Such evil shall be justified by faith, and by the forgiveness of sins.

Since Paul opposes all sex, we may imagine that—given his Jewish culture—he would be even more opposed to homosexual activity. This appears to be so:

Surely you know that the unjust will never come into possession of the kingdom of God. Make no mistake: no fornicator or

---

134. Romans 7:14-21. Even the devout Mr. Horner sees clear evidence of mental stress and confusion in this passage.

idolator, none who are guilty either of adultery or of homosexual perversion, no thieves or grabbers or drunkards or slanderers or swindlers, will possess the kingdom of God.[135]

The phrase "homosexual perversion" hides two original Greek words: *malakos* and *arsenokoites*. The word *malakos*, as every scholar of Greek knows, denotes effeminate or passive homosexuals, while *arsenokoites* (a rarer term) denotes the active counterpart. Thus an accurate English translation of the Biblical Greek would simply refer to "those who are guilty of adultery, or those males who are guilty of passive *or* active sexual intercourse with other males."[136]

We all know that the law is an excellent thing, provided we treat it as law, recognizing that it is not aimed at good citizens, but at

---

135. I Corinthians 6:9-10.

136. Johansson, Warren: "*Ex Parte Themis*: The Historical Guilt of the Christian Church," in *Homosexuality, Intolerance, and Christianity* (Gay Academic Union, New York, 1981). Cf. Horner, Tom and Houser, Ward: "New Testament" in the *Encyclopedia of Homosexuality*, p. 898. See also Wright, D. F.: "Homosexuals or Prostitutes? The Meaning of Arsenokoitai (1 *Cor.* 6:9, 1 *Tim.* 1:10)," *Vigilae Christianae* 38 (1984), 125-53. In response to Boswell's most extreme claims, on p. 333, that "the early Christian church does not appear to have opposed homosexual behavior *per se* [and that] the most influential Christian literature was moot on the issue [sic]," Wright notes that "a long list of Christian writers in East and West depict homosexual intercourse as in conflict with man's created nature....Tertullian, *Cor.* 6, *Pudic.* 4:5; Lactantius, *Div. Inst.* 6:23; Ambrose, *Abraham* 1:6:52; Pelagius and Ambrosiaster in their commentaries on *Rom.* 1:26-27; Salvian, *Gubern. Dei* 7:80; Athenagoras, *Suppl.* 34; Clement, *Paid.* 2:83 ff.; Methodius, *Symp.* 5:5; Eusebius, *Dem. Ev.* 1:6, *Laus Const.* 13:11, *Theoph.* 2:81 etc.; *Apost. Const.* 6:28:1-3, 7:2:10; Chrysostom, *Homil. on Gen.* 43:4; *De Fato et Provid.* 4, *Homil. on Rom.* 4:1-3 (more clearly than in Boswell's selective translation, pp. 359-362); *Acts of Thomas* (ed. Klijn, p. 94); Ephraim, *Hymns on Nativity* 1; Hesychius of Jerusalem and Procopius of Gaza in their commentaries on Leviticus (*PG* 93, 1015, 1046; 87, 765-6), Cyril of Alexandria, *De Adoratione* 1 (*PG* 68, 172). This is certainly an incomplete list."

the lawless and unruly, the impious and sinful, the irreligious and worldly; at parricides and matricides, murderers and fornicators, perverts [*arsenokoitai*], kidnappers, liars, perjurors—in fact all those whose behavior flouts the wholesome teaching which conforms with the gospel entrusted to me....[137]

In consequence, I say, God has given them up to shameful passions. Their women have exchanged natural intercourse for unnatural, and their men in turn, giving up natural relations with women, burn with lust for one another; males behave indecently with males, and are paid in their own persons the fitting wage of such perversion.[138]

---

137. I Timothy 1:10.
138. Romans 1:26-27. It should be noted that the remarks about women may not refer to lesbianism at all, but rather to some fancied intercourse of women with evil spirits.

It seems clear that St. Paul explicitly condemned all homosexual behavior. He termed it a kind of injustice, and established the penalty for such misconduct: hellfire.

It seems equally clear that some gay Christian activists are upset by these facts, and seek to deny the unambiguous meaning of the texts.

The situation is curious.[139]

---

139. Perhaps just as curious is Paul's personal circumcision of the young Saint Timothy (Acts 16:1-3). A curious fact (not often mentioned by modern adherents of Reformed Judaism) is that the Jewish ritual involved the *mohel*, or circumcisor, sucking the wounded member to remove the blood from the wound. This blood was known as *covenental blood*. The act (termed *mezizah*, "sucking") endured until the early nineteenth century. The antiquity of the practice is attested by the *Babylonian Talmud*: "MISHNAH: We perform all the requirements of circumcision on the Sabbath. We circumcise, uncover, suck, and place a compress and cummin upon it."[2] The *Mishnah* is the central part of the Talmud, the sacred oral history upon which the entire Rabbinic commentary is based. This was incorporated in written form well before the birth of Jesus and St. Paul. As a result, since Paul circumcised Timothy, there is no doubt that he also sucked the covenental blood from Timothy's injured member. Timothy, by all accounts, was a fully developed youth, an adolescent of remarkable charismatic qualities. (I must thank Stephen Wayne Foster for bringing these curious facts to my attention.)

Animal Allegories

As St. Paul and his new Christian faith began to make headway in the worlds of Palestine and Rome, a bizarre strain of homophobic thought emerged from the home of Christianity—the Alexandria of the Hellenized Jews of the Diaspora.

The author of *The Epistle of Barnabas* was a Jewish Christian attempting to deal with the council of 49 AD—the council which declared that the Mosaic law was no longer binding on Gentile converts to Christianity. Since almost all Christians at this time were Jews, they had a theological difficulty: they still held the Old Testament to be the word of God. Whether Jewish Christians kept the dietary laws or not, they suddenly found a need to explain them away. The most popular means of accomplishing this was to allegorize them out of existence, and this was the task of the author of *The Epistle Of Barnabas*.

The actual words of Leviticus read as follows:

> The LORD spoke to Moses and Aaron and said, Speak to the Israelites in these words: Of all animals on land these are the creatures you may eat: you may eat any animal which has a parted foot or a cloven hoof and also chews the cud; those which have only a cloven hoof or only chew the cud you may not eat. These are: the camel, because it chews the cud but has not a cloven hoof; you shall regard it as unclean; the rock-badger, because it chews the cud and has not a parted foot; you shall

regard it as unclean; the hare, because it chews the cud [sic] but has not a parted foot; you shall regard it as unclean; the pig, because it has a parted foot and a cloven hoof but does not chew the cud; you shall regard it as unclean.[140]

The literal meaning of this text is clear, but the times demanded an allegorical explanation of these rules, which developed along the following lines: God actually meant that each of the listed unclean animals was an evil animal, and we should not imitate their evil ways. Thus, we should not *act* like pigs; pigs have evil ways. This upsets the meaning of the original completely, which is one of the goals of allegorical exegesis.

Here is the resolution offered by *The Epistle of Barnabas*:

> But why did Moses say Ye shall not eat of the swine, neither the eagle or the hawk; nor the crow; nor any fish that has not a scale upon him?—answer, that in the spiritual sense, he comprehended three doctrines, that were to be gathered from thence.
>
> Besides which he says to them in the book of Deuteronomy [but not in Leviticus], And I will give my statutes unto this people. Wherefore it is not the command of God that they should not eat these things; but Moses in the spirit spake unto them.

---

140. Leviticus 11:1-8.

Now the sow he forbade them to eat; meaning thus much; thou shalt not join thyself to such persons as are like unto swine; who whilst they live in pleasure, forget their God; but when any want pinches them, then they know the Lord; as the sow when she is full knows not her master; but when she is hungry she makes a noise; and being again fed, is silent....

But he adds, neither shalt thou eat of the hare. To what end?—To signify this to us: Thou shalt not be a boy-molester; nor liken thyself to such persons. For the hare every year multiplies its anuses; and so many years as it lives, so many it has [sic].

Neither shalt thou eat of the hyena [an animal not specified by Moses]; that is, again, be not an adulterer, nor a seducer; neither be like to such. And wherefore so?—Because that creature every year changes its kind, and is sometimes male and sometimes female [sic].

For which cause he also justly hated the weasel; to the end that they should not be like such persons who with their mouths commit wickedness by reason of their uncleanness [a reference to fellatio]; nor join themselves with impure women, who with their mouths commit wickedness. Because that animal conceives with its mouth [sic].[141]

---

141. *The Epistle of Barnabas* 9:1-9 in *The Lost Books of the Bible and the Forgotten Books of Eden* (New American Library, 1974, paperback). Translation emended following Boswell and others.

Even in the context of allegory, there is room for some surprise here: clearly the author had never seen a hare, or had never examined one with any care. A minimal amount of empirical investigation would have revealed the biological pitfalls in this text. But, unfortunately, as we move into the world of late antiquity, we are rapidly leaving such trivial things as scientific proof behind us. The standard of truth is becoming the holy scripture and anything which can be deduced from it. Rabbi Nachmanides did indeed say of Aristotle "May his name be erased." There was also a Jewish teaching which condemned the eating of pork and the teaching of Greek science in the same breath.[142] Whatever the justified claims of the Christian Revolution, we will never be able to say that it was scientific.

Thus the words of Barnabas were never verified; they were only transcribed and elaborated.

Aside from the author's dishonesty and ignorance, his homophobia is also painfully clear: he is obviously glad to find another weapon to hurl at homosexuals. This poppycock about the hyena and the hare actually made a hit; it caught on. It echoed down the centuries as part of the litany of standard accusations against the lovers of their own sex. Clement of Alexandria repeated the charge, as we shall see in the next chapter.

Another formulation from the Hebrew Apocrypha seems also to have gained wide popularity: "Become not as Sodom, which changed the order of nature."[143]

---

142. This peculiar proscription is recorded by Renan: *Life of Jesus*, p. 91 of the Modern Library edition, in Chapter III, "The Education of Jesus."

143. *The Testament of Naphtali* 1:26.

CLEMENT OF ALEXANDRIA

Clement of Alexandria (c. 150-215 AD) was a complex figure of the early Christian era. He was not only a fool and a humbug—he was also a liar and a thief.

Sober historians do not normally render such negative judgements (in print, at any rate), but with Clement there appears to be little choice—his stupidity is an open secret among professional historians. The roster of Roman Catholic saints *who have later been stripped of their sainthood* is a short one indeed, but Clement is on it. (He was "un-sainted" in 1586, because some of his views appeared to be unorthodox.)

Nevertheless, he was a very influential preacher and theologian: he continued the attempt to reconcile Greek philosophy with the laws of Moses, and laid the groundwork for the doctrinal developments and disputes of the next three centuries. He was the teacher of Origen the eunuch, and he was a saint for well over a thousand years.

One of his unorthodox views was that he, himself, was a perfect human being, and therefore well able to discuss and chastise the sins of his lesser fellows, the imperfect men who surrounded him.

He deduced his own perfection from a strict interpretation of the doctrine of baptism, which holds that those who believe and are baptized shall be saved.

This is what happens with us, whose model the Lord made Himself. When we are baptized, we are enlightened; being enlightened, we become adopted sons; becoming adopted sons, we are made perfect; and becoming perfect, we are made divine. "I have said," it is written, "you are gods and all of you sons of the most High."[144]

While committing this proud blunder, Clement misquotes scripture. His citation is annotated by the frustrated Catholic translators as Psalms 82:6, but Psalm 82 presents God speaking to other gods:

This is my sentence: Gods you may be, sons all of you of a high god, yet you shall die as men die; princes fall, every one of them, and so shall you.

This has no relation at all to Clement's doctrine that baptism brings about human perfection on earth.

However, it is Clement's doctrine, and from this follows Clement's belief in his own perfection—this is what accounts for his characteristically patronizing and condescending attitude. A perfect human being does not need to verify sources, or reconcile doctrines.

---

144. Clement, *Christ the Educator* (which is the *Paidagogos*), trans. Simon Wood, in *Fathers of the Church*, volume 23, p. 26 (New York, 1954).

Clement misquotes Plato, he misquotes Moses, and he claims to be constructing a synthesis between the two. In this, he follows the tradition of Philo, but there is worse to Clement than this unpredictable lurching about—he is also a thief.

As devoutly Christian sources tell it:

> Even more damaging to Clement's reputation is the accusation made by Wendland and seconded by Parker, that books 2-3 of the *Paidagogos* are nothing but a worked-over copy of Musonius, the Stoic teacher of Epictetus. It is a charge that would surely undermine Clement's integrity and the value of the work. However, while there are clear proofs that Clement did use Musonius, both in general arrangement and in many details, such an arbitrary method of higher criticism cannot be taken seriously.[145]

It may seem difficult to believe that Clement could misquote the Ten Commandments, yet here he is:

> Moses forbade, too, in clear language and with his head uncovered, no longer under a figure: "Thou shalt not fornicate, nor commit adultery, nor corrupt boys."[146]

---

145. *Paidagogos*, p. xvii. It seems to me that these commentators, while trying to save poor Clement, only manage to dig him into deeper trouble.

146. *Paidagogos*, p. 168.

This is annotated, in *The Fathers of the Church*, as "Cf. Exod. 20:14; *Ep. of Barn.* 19.4."[147] The reference in Exodus is right in the middle of the Ten Commandments, and only adultery is on that list. "Corrupting boys"—*paidophthoria*, a word newly coined by Christians to replace the nobler *paiderastia*[148]—certainly is not on that list, and neither is fornication. *Barnabas* only contains the story of the hare and the hyena, where, if Moses spoke at all, he most certainly spoke "under a figure."

Thus it becomes clear that there is no Biblical source at all for this dictum which Clement pops into the mouth of Moses: he stitched it together himself in his own theology-shop.

On top of these failings, he is often incomprehensible. As his sometimes exasperated translator, the intrepid Simon Wood, notes:

> Clement often piles up impressive quotations that do not clearly apply to the point under discussion; he sometimes does not make one point fully before passing on to another point whose connection is not easy to grasp; occasionally he contradicts himself.... These traits evidently exasperated E. Molland, for he claims that Clement is one of the most difficult authors in the whole Christian literature, and that he had no theological system at all. In fact, Molland quotes Julicher approvingly as saying that the reason Clement was not repudiated as a heretic in the fifth and sixth centuries is the fact that he was unintelligible.[149]

---

147. Barnabas does not contain a chapter 19; the reference is to the material in chapter 9 we have just reviewed.

148. Brandt/Licht, p. 414.

149. *Paidagogos*, p. xiii.

All of the failings listed above are on display in Clement's *Paidagogos*, where he summarizes his feelings about homosexual behavior. Although the following extract from that work is replete with faults, including bad citations, inaccurate readings, and inimitable errors of logic and inference, it is important to remember the enormous influence of Clement's work—for more than a millenium, the teachings of Clement were regarded as only a bit less reliable than the word of God.

> It remains for us now to consider the restriction of sexual intercourse to those who are joined in wedlock. Begetting children is the goal of those who wed, and the fulfillment of that goal is a large family, just as hope of a crop drives the farmer to sow his seed, while the fulfillment of his hope is the actual harvesting of the crop. But he who sows in a living soil is far superior, for the one tills the land to provide food only for a season, the other to secure the preservation of the whole human race;[150] the one tends his crop for himself, the other, for God. We have received the command: "Be fruitful," and we must obey. In this role, man becomes like God, because he cooperates, in his human way, in the birth of another man.
>
> Now, not every land is suited to the reception of seed, and, even if it were, not at the hands of the same farmer. Seed should not

---

150. The careful reader will note that this typically Clementine argument is wholly invalid; the absence of food would quickly wipe out the human race, and both parts of the equation are equally necessary for any successful population.

be sown on rocky ground[151] nor scattered everywhere, for it is the primary substance of generation and contains imbedded in itself the principle of nature. It is undeniably godless, then, to dishonor principles of nature by wasting them on unnatural resting places. In fact, you recall how Moses, in his wisdom, once denounced seed that bears no fruit, saying symbolically: "Do not eat the hare nor the hyena."[152] He does not want man to be contaminated by their traits nor even to taste of their wantonness, for these animals have an insatiable appetite for coition. As regards the hare, legend claims that it needs to void excrement only once a year,[153] and possesses as many anuses as the years it has lived. Therefore, the prohibition against eating the hare is nothing else than a condemnation of pederasty.[154] And with regard to the hyena, it is said that the male changes every year into a female, so that Moses means that he who abstains from the hyena is commanded not to lust after adultery.

While I agree that the all-wise Moses means, by this prohibition, just mentioned, that we should not become like these beasts, I do not entirely agree with the explanation given these symbolic prohibitions. A nature can never be made to change; what has been once formed in it cannot be reformed by any sort of change.[155] Change does not involve the nature itself; it necessarily modifies,

---

151. Clement is repeating Plato: *Laws* 839a.

152. This is, of course, the mythical Moses of *Barnabas*.

153. This must be Clement's own legend, since anyone who has owned a hare has other ideas on the matter.

154. The "therefore" is vintage Clement.

155. Neo-Platonic verbalism at its worst. Whatever Clement means, he is refuted by the metamorphosis of a caterpillar into a butterfly.

but does not transform the structure. For instance, although many birds are said to change their color and their voice according to the season...even so, their nature itself is not so affected that a male becomes a female. Rather, a new growth of feathers, like a new garment, is bright with one color, but a little later, as winter threatens, it fades away, like a flower when its color goes. In the same way, the voice, affected unfavorably by the cold, loses its vibrancy....Later on, in the spring, responding to the weather and relaxing, the breath is once again freed...No longer does the voice croak in dying tones, but bursts forth clear, pouring out in full-throated voice, and now in springtime there arises melodious song from the throats of the birds.

Therefore,[156] we should not believe at all that the hyena changes its sex. Neither does it possess both the male and female sexual organs at the same time, as some claim, conjuring up some freakish hermaphrodite and creating this female-male, a third new category halfway in between the male and the female. Erroneously they misconstrue the strategy of nature, mother of all and author of all existence.[157] Because the hyena is of all animals the most sensual, there is a knob of flesh under its tail, in front of the anus, closely resembling the female organ in shape. It is not a passage, I mean it serves no useful purpose, opening

---

156. See note 154.

157. Erroneously does Clement misconstrue the strategy of nature, if there be one, for it is by now common knowledge that the animal universe contains a wide range of hermaphroditism. Also noteworthy is the assimilation of "nature" to "God," the latter being the traditional "author of all existence."

neither into the womb nor into the intestines. It has only a good-sized opening to permit an ineffective sexual act when the vagina is preparing for childbirth and is impenetrable. This is characteristic of both male and female hyena, because of their hyperactive abnormal sexuality; the male lies with the male so that it rarely approaches the female. For that reason, births are infrequent among hyenas,[158] because they so freely sow their seed contrary to nature.

This is the reason, I believe, that Plato, in excoriating pederasty in *Phaedrus,* terms it bestiality, and says that these libertines who have so surrendered to pleasure, "taking the bit in their own mouths, like brutish beasts rush on to enjoy and beget."[159] Such godless people "God has given over," the Apostle says, "to shameful lusts. For the women change their natural use to that which is against nature, and in like manner the men, also, having abandoned the natural use of the women, have burned in their lusts towards one another, men with men doing shameful things, and receiving in themselves the fitting recompense of their perversity."[160] Yet, nature has not allowed even the most sensual of beasts to sexually misuse the passage made for excrement.[161] Urine she gathers into the bladder; undigested food in the intestines; tears in the eyes; blood in the veins; wax in the ear, and

---

158. [sic]—argument now from Philo.
159. A violent twisting of Plato's words, indeed. The *Phaedrus* is a long hymn in favor of pederasty, and an anatomy of the human soul, with the human charioteer guiding the famous white and black horses; the white horse represents virtue and chaste love, while the black horse represents lusty desires and is to be controlled by the charioteer. *Nowhere*, of course, does Plato assimilate pederasty to "bestiality."
160. St. Paul, of course.
161. The most sensual of beasts is, of course, the hyena.

mucous in the nose; so, too, there is a passage connected to the end of the intestines by means of which excrement is passed off. In the case of hyenas, nature, in her diversity, has added this additional organ to accommodate their excessive sexual activity. Therefore, it is large enough for the service of the lusting organs, but its opening is obstructed within. In short, it is not made to serve any purpose in generation.[162] The clear conclusion we must draw, then, is that we must condemn sodomy, all fruitless sowing of seed, any unnatural methods of holding intercourse and the reversal of the sexual role in intercourse. We must rather follow the guidance of nature, which obviously disapproves of such practices from the very way she has fashioned the male organ, adapted not for receiving the seed, but for implanting it. When Jeremias, or rather, the Spirit through him, said "The cave of the hyena is my home," He was resorting to an expressive figure to excoriate idolatry and to manifest His scorn for the nourishment provided for dead bodies. The house of the living God surely ought to be free of idols.[163]

Again, Moses issued a prohibition against eating the hare. The hare is forever mounting the female, leaping upon her crouching form from behind. In fact, this manner of having intercourse is a characteristic of the hare. The female conceives every month,

---

162. It also does not exist, but perhaps that is irrelevant by now.
163. Clement has clearly lost the thread of his argument at this point.

and, even before the first offspring is born, she becomes pregnant again. She conceives and begets, and as soon as she gives birth is fertilized again by the first hare she meets. Not satisfied with one mate, she conceives again, although she is still nursing. The explanation for this is that a female hare has a double womb, and therefore her desire for intercourse is stimulated not only by the emptiness of the womb, in that every empty space seeks to be filled, but also, when she is with young, her other womb begins to feel lustful desires. That is why hares have one birth after another. So the mysterious prohibition [of Moses] in reality is but counsel to restrain violent sexual impulses, and intercourse in too frequent succession, relations with a pregnant woman, pederasty, adultery, and lewdness.

Moses forbade, too, in clear language and with his head uncovered, no longer under a figure: "Thou shalt not fornicate, nor commit adultery, nor corrupt boys."[164] This is the command of the Word; it must be obeyed with all our strength and not transgressed in any way; His commandments may not be set aside. Evil lust bears the name wantonness; Plato, for example, calls the horse representing lust "wanton" when he writes "You have become in my eyes horses mad for the female."[165] The angels who visited Sodom reveal the punishment reserved for

---

164. See the discussion earlier; Clement is improving the Ten Commandments to his own taste.

165. The citation is from the Old Testament, *not* Plato. *Jeremiah* 5:8.

wantonness. They struck down with fire those who attempted to dishonor them, and their city along with them. Such a deed demonstrates clearly that fire is the reward of wantonness. As we have already said, the calamities that befell the ancients are described for our instruction that we may not imitate their example and merit the same punishment.

We should consider boys as our sons, and the wives of other men as our daughters. We must keep a firm control over the pleasures of the stomach, and an absolutely uncompromising control over the organs beneath the stomach. If, as the Stoics teach, we should not move even a finger on mere impulse, how much more necessary is it that they who seek wisdom control the organ of intercourse? I feel that the reason this organ is also called the private part is that we are to treat it with privacy and modesty more than we do any other member. In lawful wedlock, as with eating, nature permits whatever is conformable to nature and helpful and decent; whoever is guilty of excess sins against nature and, by violating the laws regulating intercourse, harms himself. First of all, it is decidedly wrong ever to touch youths in any sexual way as though they were girls. The philosopher that learned from Moses[166] taught: "Do not sow seeds on rocks and stones, on which they will never take root."[167] The Word, too, commands

---

166. This would be Plato. A common misconception of the time was that Moses had instructed Plato.

167. An accurate citation! *Laws* 839a.

emphatically, "Thou shalt not lie with mankind as with womankind, for it is an abomination."[168] Again, further on, noble Plato advises: "Abstain from every female field of increase," because it does not belong to you. (He had read this in the holy Scriptures [sic] and from it taken the Law: "Thou shalt not give the coition of thy seed to thy neighbor's wife, to be defiled because of her.")[169] He then goes on to say: "Do not sow the unconsecrated and bastard seed with concubines, where you would not want what is sown to grow."[170] In fact, he says: "Do not touch anyone, except your own wedded wife,"[171] because she is the only one with whom it is lawful to enjoy the pleasures of the flesh for the purpose of begetting lawful heirs.[172]

Though Clement is an unreliable and chaotic author, he does present us with another element in the developing pattern of Christian texts: the arguments against homosexuality are mustered from every corner of the earth, and combined in a "synthesis" of homophobia. I cannot think of a source Clement has overlooked—Leviticus, Plato, the grand myth of Sodom, the arguments from Philo, the anathema of St. Paul, and the latest wrinkle in animal physiology from *The Epistle of Barnabas*. Typically, he adds some of his own poison to the brew, but his main object is to fling every bit of holy mud available to him.

---

168. Leviticus, of course.
169. Leviticus 18:20.
170. A misquotation of the passage just transcribed from Plato.
171. *Laws* 841d.
172. *Paidagogos*, pp. 164-70.

In modern times, it matters little that Clement *also* said that the Thessalians worship ants,[173] and that his rule of unreason drove his translator to remark, in a footnote: "For once, Clement's etymological analysis is correct." What does matter is that he was a Saint; he had a vast influence on the development of Christian theology; and the sexual policy of the modern Catholic church is indistinguishable from the policy of "the gentle Clement."

---

173. Clement: *Exhortation to the Heathen*, in *The Anti-Nicene Fathers*, volume ii, ed. Roberts and Donaldson, p. 182 (Grand Rapids, 1956).

The Triumph of Fanaticism

The Roman world, violent and cruel though it was, was not originally a fanatical place—fanaticism, for the present purposes, being defined as the belief that religion is the most important thing in the world, coupled with the belief that one is in possession of the true religion.

This sort of fanaticism seems to have originated with the Jews or the Persians, and was also a distinguishing mark of Judaism's two daughter-religions—Christianity and Islam. As we move further into Late Antiquity, this pattern of behavior is more often observed within the Roman Empire.

It began simply enough, when the earliest Christians refused to offer the traditional pinch of incense to the statue of the "divine emperor." This trivial and traditional Roman gesture was more a mark of patriotism than of any real religious feeling, but to the Christians (and the Jews before them) it was something utterly forbidden by the Ten Commandments: "Thou shalt have no other gods before me."

This refusal was interpreted by the Romans as a lack of patriotism, who were further shocked by the Christians' absolute refusal of military service. This was something new to the average Roman, and it was perceived as "atheism" (in the very limited Roman sense), a lack of loyalty, and cowardice. Puzzled governors (such as Pliny) sent letters back to Rome asking for guidance in dealing with such offenders. For the first 250 years of the Christian church, the actions of the emperors were largely protective of the Christians: real persecutions and torment came from the active demand of their fellow citizens, and were sporadic.[174]

The reign of Diocletian (285-305 AD) brought fundamental changes to the empire, which had very nearly collapsed. Diocletian replaced the imperial power structure and began the custom of referring to the emperor as *dominus* ("Lord"), and treating him as a living god. He established a proto-Byzantine system of rule, and wore a tiara of precious metals and gems; his very shoes were encrusted with priceless jewels. He removed the capital from Rome to Milan, and instituted various demoralizing social "reforms," such as fixing prices and wages, and tying farmers to the land.

To preserve the empire, his tetrarchy, and himself, Diocletian was ready to do many unsavory deeds. He had no objection to religious persecution—he ordered the leaders of the Manichean sect burned alive together with their scriptures; their followers were beheaded or condemned to the mines, and their property was claimed by the imperial treasury.

At the end of his reign, pressured by Galerius, Diocletian unleashed the most violent persecution the Christians had ever known. In the years 303-4, edicts of increasing severity ordered the destruction of churches, seizure of scriptures, imprisonment of priests, and a sentence of death for all those who refused to sacrifice to the Roman gods. In the East, where Galerius reigned, the persecution was shockingly violent, especially in Egypt and Palestine. In Italy, Maximian showed himself less zealous, and in Gaul,

---

174. Fox, Robin Lane: *Pagans and Christians*, p. 450 (New York, 1986).

Constantius (the father of Constantine) limited himself to the destruction of a few churches as a token obedience. But in the East, the persecution lasted as late as the year 312.

Fanaticism seems to beget fanaticism. The initial Christian refusal to sacrifice to idols resulted in horrific religious persecutions, and also in a surprising rise in *pagan fanaticism.* The wholly fictitious *Life of Apollonius of Tyana*, by Philostratus, was an attempt to set up a pagan counter-example to the Christ of the New Testament. Apollonius spoke with the pagan gods, worked miracles, and was in many respects similar to Jesus. This represents a curious failure of pagan philosophy: rather than simply asserting the impossibility of miracles, the pagans began claiming that they could work miracles as well as any Christian.

Perhaps it was the "death wish of a civilization," perhaps it was a "failure of the intellectual classes," perhaps it was neither. But the rational universe was being rapidly abandoned on all sides. The late Roman philosopher Plotinus is an example of this tendency: he developed a very elaborate scheme for the whole realm of being, not one particle of which was open to impartial verification. He is still cited with fondness by our modern doctors of divinity and theology. Gibbon said it well:

> The declining age of learning and of mankind is marked…by the rise and rapid progress of the new Platonists.…Several of these masters, Ammonius, Plotinus, Amelius, and Porphyry, were men of profound thought and intense application; but, by mistaking the true object of philosophy, their labours contributed much less to improve than to corrupt the human understanding. The knowledge that is suited to our situation and powers, the whole compass of moral, natural and mathematical science, was neglected by the new Platonists, whilst they exhausted their strength in the verbal disputes of metaphysics, attempted to explore the secrets of the invisible world, and studied to reconcile Aristotle with Plato, on subjects of which both

these philosophers were as ignorant as the rest of mankind. Consuming their reason in these deep but unsubstantial meditations, their minds were exposed to illusions of fancy. They flattered themselves that they possessed the secret of disengaging the soul from its corporeal prison; claimed a familiar intercourse with daemons and spirits; and, by a very singular revolution, converted the study of philosophy into that of magic.... The new Platonists would scarcely deserve a place in the history of science, but in that of the church the mention of them will very frequently occur.[175]

The evidence for the philosophers is not complete. Like Diocletian, the early Christians turned their enemies, and their enemies' books, into ashes. Celsus' *The True Teaching* and Porphyry's *Against the Christians* are two philosophical arguments against the new faith which have not survived, and they may have been dangerous. It would be interesting to know, but we do not.

---

175. Gibbon, vol. I, chap. xiii, pp. 423-4.

The Conversion of Constantine

The events between the year 312 AD and the fall of Rome are crucial to the arguments developed in this book, but the historical record now presents a difficulty. These years are commonly ignored; the late Roman Empire is a little-visited backwater of Western history.

Who knows, or cares to know, of Jovian, Theodosius, Julian and the rest? Very few. The reason, it seems to me, is not "enforced amnesia"—though that may have played a part—but a simple principle of human psychology: no one enjoys reading stories where *all* the characters are evil. Wise authors know better than to invent a fiction with no hero, no protagonist.

But the history of the final years of the Western Roman Empire is not fiction, and it needs to be examined here.

Constantine seized control of the Empire with his historic victory in the battle of the Milvian Bridge: he was already perceived by many as a young hero galloping out of the West to stop the horrible persecutions of Christians in the Eastern empire.[176]

During this battle, legend tells us, Constantine had a vision of the cross leading him to victory, and received the supernatural message "In This Sign Shall You Conquer."

---

176. Barnes, Timothy B.: *Constantine and Eusebius*, pp. 43 and 75, among others (Cambridge, 1981). Another good source for this era is Lot, Ferdinand: *The End of the Ancient World and the Beginnings of the Middle Ages* (New York, 1931; paperback reprint 1961).

He was attended by many learned and influential Christians, who assisted his conversion to the new faith. A year later, Constantine issued the Edict of Milan, which provided for universal religious toleration. This exemplary law, in retrospect, was a mere tactical maneuver, for the emperor quickly demonstrated that one particular religion was much more equal than the others. His favorable policy towards the Christian church never wavered. The recently persecuted church was showered with favors and grew magnificently wealthy. Great basilicas were constructed at Rome and Constantinople, the imperial treasury gave liberal donations and grants to the church, the clergy were exempted from taxes, bishops were given judicial authority, and exceptional promotions were given to Christian officials.

Although Constantine retained the pagan title of *pontifex maximus*, he spoke of pagans with contempt, and by 324 his imperial voice was echoing his personal contempt. Christianity was proclaimed to be the official religion of the empire, and throughout the East persecuted Christians took bloody revenge on those who had tormented them.

Constantine specifically forbade the erection of pagan religious statues, the consultation of oracles, pagan divination of any sort, and sacrifice to the gods under any circumstances. This was a sudden and profound shock to the pagan belief-system, the mirror image of the shock felt by the Christians when Diocletian loosed his hounds of war upon them, and Constantine never wavered—pagan sacrifice remained completely forbidden for the rest of his reign.[177]

The anti-pagan policy was also a fiscal policy: special committees were sent to all the Eastern provinces, where they seized any gold, silver or jewels found in pagan shrines. The proceeds were enormous: forty

---

177. Barnes, p. 83.

years later, an author claimed that gold was once again in circulation for the smallest transactions.[178]

The judicial authority given to bishops was extraordinary. The law held that any Christian engaged in any legal action could at any time (even without the consent of the judge or the opposing party) transfer the case to the arbitration of a bishop, whose decision would be final, not subject to any appeal or revision.[179]

Constantine also convened and presided over the Council of Nicea, where an early version of the Nicene Creed was hammered out, and Arius was declared a heretic.

(The Arian heresy will recur: Arius held that Jesus was not God, but a special emanation from God, while Athanasius held that Jesus and God were the same being. The "Arian heresy" was most fully developed by the Muslims in later centuries.)

The reign of Constantine also saw the sexual code of the Christian church written into the books of Roman law. The law of marriage was fundamentally changed. The Roman law had been geared towards ensuring a large progeny; the Christian law was geared towards *virginity*, more admired than any other attribute. The Roman law, for example, prevented childless people from inheriting anything: Constantine removed that restriction. Divorce became much more difficult: the only grounds for a woman were murder, poisoning, and tomb violation, while the male could

---

[178]. Barnes, p. 247.
[179]. Barnes, p. 51. This law *may* have applied only to cases where both litigants were Christian.

only sue for adultery, poisoning, and being able to prove that his wife was running a brothel.

In 326, the new laws were further elaborated. Married men were forbidden to have concubines. When a girl wished to marry, her ward had to furnish proof that she was a virgin, or face deportation and confiscation of property. Rapists were punished by being burned alive, with no appeal possible. An eloping couple were faced with the same penalty, and nurses who encouraged girls to elope were to have boiling lead poured down their throats. Anyone who aided such eloping couples would likewise be burned alive.

> Constantine treated seduction like a ritual impurity which can in no way be cleansed. If parents of virgins who had been seduced concealed the crime, they became liable to deportation, and any slave who reported their attempts at concealment received a reward. Even a virgin who was violently raped deserved punishment, since she could have stayed safely at home. Professing clemency, the Emperor ordained that she should lose the right to inherit property from her parents—and hence, presumably, any chance of a dowry and a respectable husband.[180]

The engine behind all these radical transformations was undergoing changes himself. The youthful hero of the Milvian Bridge gradually

---

180. Barnes, p. 220.

became a bizarre fantasy figure of Byzantine pomp, loaded with wealth and jewelry, wearing false hair of various colors, laboriously arranged, and dressed in elaborate robes of silk embroidered with flowers of gold. As he slowly took leave of the real world, he arranged to murder his son, his wife and his nephew.

His son Crispus was a very popular figure, and may have been seen as a threat. A charge of adultery was trumped up, and the father executed his own son.

He stuffed his wife into a superheated bath and steamed her to death. Then he killed his nephew.[181]

Constantine also launched the first wave of official Christian anti-Semitism. Jerusalem became a Christian city, and the Jews were permitted to enter only on one day each year, in order to bewail their fate. Jews were forbidden to own Christian slaves, and were forbidden to proselytize—in fact, they were forbidden to accept converts. Any Jew who attempted to prevent conversions to Christianity was to be burned alive. Constantine, along with Eusebius, was responsible for imperial propaganda to the effect that the destruction of the Temple in 68 AD was an act of divine retribution for the Jews, who had failed to recognize the true messiah. The Roman lawbooks begin referring to the Jews as a "feral sect."[182]

In the year 337, Constantine received the rite of baptism and died.[183] Five years after his death, his Christian sons issued the following edict:

---

181. Gibbon, vol. 2, chap. 18. Barnes, pp. 220-1.

182. Phare, Clyde (trans.): *The Theodosian Code*, 16.8.1, p. 467 (New York, 1952).

183. As we have seen, the early Christians had different ideas about baptism. Many delayed the rite, fearing that any sin committed after receiving it would irrevocably damn the purified soul.

The Emperors Constantius and Constans Augustus to the People.

When a man submits to men, the way a woman does, what can he be seeking? where sex has lost its proper place? where the crime is one it is not profitable to know? where Venus is changed into another form? where love is sought and does not appear? We order statutes to arise, and the laws to be armed with an avenging sword, that those guilty of such infamous crimes, either now or in the future, may be subjected to exquisite penalties.

Given on the day before the nones of December at Milan— December 4. Posted at Rome on the seventeenth day before the kalends of January in the year of the third consulship of Constantius Augustus and the second consulship of Constans Augustus. December 16, 342.[184]

This law is the first part of the implementation of the anti-homosexual regime of the Christian church—the first law against homosexual behavior ever seen in the Mediterranean world outside of Palestine. The Gentiles were a bit slow in realizing that the new Hebrew code encompassed *all* homosexual activity, however. The first law does the obvious thing: it provides the death penalty for conspicuous homosexuals. But the male brothels remained in place, and the emperors continued

---

184. *Theodosian Code*, 9.7.3, p. 467. Translation emended following Lauritsen, John: "*Culpa Ecclesiæ*: Boswell's Dilemma," in *Homosexuality, Intolerance, and Christianity* (Gay Academic Union, New York, 1981). Compare the language at 9.16.4.

receiving the brothel tax receipts, until Theodosius enacted the definitive law in 390 AD.

This second law exists in a short form and a long form. Here is the shorter version:

> All persons who have the shameful custom of condemning a man's body, acting the part of a woman's, to the sufferance of an alien sex (for they appear not to be different from women), shall expiate a crime of this kind in avenging flames in the sight of the people. (August 6, 390)
>
> [Interpretation]: This law does not require interpretation.[185]

Here is the longer version:

> OF DEBAUCHERS
>
> Moses says:
>
> If anyone hath intercourse with a male as with a woman, it is an abomination. Let them both die; they are guilty....
>
> This indeed is the law. But a constitution of the Emperor Theodosius followed to the full the spirit of the Mosaic Law. (Likewise the Theodosian Code).:

---

185. *Theodosian Code*, 9.7.3, p. 232.

THE EMPERORS VALENTINIAN, THEODOSIUS AND ARCADIUS, TO ORIENTIUS, THE VICAR OF THE CITY OF ROME:

We shall not suffer the City of Rome, the mother of all virtues, any longer to be defiled by the pollution of effeminacy in males and the rustic vigor inherited from her founding fathers, weakened through the unmanliness of her people, to become a reproach for the ages either to her founder or to her rulers. O Orientius whom we love and cherish, praiseworthy therefore is your practice of seizing all who have committed the crime of treating their male bodies as though they were female, submitting them to the use becoming the opposite sex, and being in no wise distinguishable from a woman, and—as the monstrosity of the crime demands—dragging them out of the brothels (it is shameful to say) for males…in the sight of the people shall the offender expiate his crime in the avenging flames that each and every one may understand that the dwelling place of the male soul should be sacrosanct to all and that no one may without incurring the ultimate penalty aspire to play the part of another sex by shamefully renouncing his own. (May 14, 390)[186]

---

186. *Mosaicarum et Romanarum Legum Collatio* (Oxford, 1913) trans. Hyamson and Johansson, in Lauritsen, John: "*Culpa Ecclesiae*: Boswell's Dilemma" in *Homosexuality, Intolerance, and Christianity* (Gay Academic Union, New York, 1981).

So it is clear that the Roman laws regarding heterosexual and homosexual behavior were drastically altered after Christianity became the established religion of the Roman empire.

This is hardly surprising.

THE ESTABLISHMENT OF CHRISTIANITY

With the advent of Constantine, the Empire became officially Christian, and, with the brief exception of Julian, remained Christian until it collapsed. The principal emperors after Constantine were Constantius, Julian, Valentinian, Valens, and Theodosius. These emperors were plagued by internal schism as they brought about the establishment of the new religion.

They also had personal problems. As we have seen, Constantine murdered several members of his family. Constantius began his reign with a copious murder of his nearest relatives. Valentinian seems to have been a genuine sadist, who was widely reported to feed people to bears for his private amusement. Theodosius committed a mass slaughter at Thessalonica which shocked the empire. The conversion of the empire was intended to improve things, but the improvement is not apparent to the untrained eye.

The internal schism occurred between Arian and Athanasian Christians. After Constantine developed the Nicene Creed and died, Constantius (an Arian) collected another council of eminent Christians, and, at the Council of Rimini, simply cancelled the dogma elaborated at the Council of Nicea.

On Constantius' death, Julian ascended to the throne and attempted a pagan counterrevolution. During his brief reign of two years, he failed utterly. The reason is not hard to find: he failed because the people of the empire *detested him*—not for his paganism, but for his prudery.[187] Both Christians and pagans intensely disliked "the talking mole": an emperor who had given up sex entirely, a wildly religious neo-Platonic fanatic who was enthusiastically ascetic even in diet, and who was deathly afraid of the theater on moral grounds. Cavafy summed it up:[188]

Julian and the People of Antioch

> Was it ever possible that they should renounce
> their lovely way of life; the variety of their
> daily amusement; their magnificent theater
> where a union of the Arts was taking place
> with the amorous tendencies of the flesh?

> They were immoral to a point—and possibly to a great
> degree. But they had the satisfaction of knowing
> that their life was the *much talked about* life of Antioch,
> rich in pleasures, perfectly elegant in every way.

> To renounce all these, to turn to what after all?

---

187. Bowersock, G. W.: *Julian the Apostate*, pp. 1-122 (Cambridge, 1978).
188. Cavafy, C. P., trans. Rae Dalven: The Complete Poems of Cavafy, p. 137 (New York, 1961). The CHI refers to Christ, while the KAPPA refers to Constantius.

To his airy chatter about false gods;
to his tiresome self-centered chatter;
to his childish fear of the theater;
his graceless prudery; his ridiculous beard?

Ah, most certainly they preferred the CHI,
ah most certainly they preferred the KAPPA; a hundred times.

Julian was clearly not the sort of pagan to put a high priority on getting rid of the Christian legislation against homosexual behavior between males. Given time, he might have modified it, but this is speculation: he died in battle quite soon.

After the eight-month reign of Jovian, Valentinian assumed the throne. He promulgated an edict of religious toleration (for which Saint Ambrose and many Christians disliked him) and spent most of his time defending the frontiers. He was a powerful and arrogant ruler, who took nonsense from no one, and his severity was legendary: he was never known to grant a reprieve to anyone sentenced to death.[189]

---

189. An excellent source for this era is Homes Dudden, F: *The Life and Times of Saint Ambrose* (Oxford, 1935).

In 364, pressure from the army forced Valentinian to name a co-emperor, and he cynically chose his brother Valens, a man of innumerable faults who was dependably loyal, and well aware that he would never maintain power in his own right.

Valentinian spent a good deal of time outlawing magic, which makes sense in the historical context—everyone, including Christians, believed in magic and demons. In this legislation, he continued the practice of Constantine and Constantius. But Valentinian had a purpose in mind—a reign of terror against the Roman upper classes. Anyone suspected of plotting against him was arrested on grounds of practicing magic. Anonymous denunciations were accepted, and normal legal procedures were abandoned. The commissioners working for Valentinian soon learned that their job-performance was directly judged by the number of "guilty" verdicts produced. Suspects were dragged in from the farthest reaches of the empire; senators, respectable matrons, and philosophers perished under grotesque tortures.

In addition to magic, the inquisitors could also produce a charge of adultery, since Constantine had established the death penalty for this offense.[190] Such a mixture of treason and magic, poison and adultery, presented a nearly infinite number of degrees of guilt and innocence. Frightened members of the upper class were already burning books in the anticipation of arrest.

---

190. Gibbon, chap. 25.

In the East, in the meantime, Valens began his persecution of Catholic Christians, whom he called the *Athanasian heretics.*

When Valentinian died, he left the empire in the hands of incompetents: the absurd Valens went out to confront the barbarians, and managed to lose two-thirds of the Roman Army in the disastrous defeat of Hadrianople (378 AD); Valens perished in the battle, and the remaining incompetents had the sense to send for a soldier: Theodosius was quickly made a co-emperor and just as quickly began seizing control of the empire.

Already by 380, he had re-decided the Arian/Athanasian question, and written the decision into law,[191] identifying the true Christian religion as that practiced by Pope Damasus of Rome. The divisive effect of this law is shown by the preceding struggle to elect Damasus as Pope, the scandal of the age. The contest between Damasus and Ursinus provoked a bloody battle with hatchets and firebrands; when order was finally restored, a hundred and thirty-seven corpses were found on the church floor.[192]

The Theodosian legislation in favor of the Athanasians never abated; he issued seventeen laws denying property, churches and life to all who refused to accept the Nicene creed. The persecution of Christian heretics was ferocious. The Spaniard ascetic Priscillian was denounced as a manifest heretic, and, being a very devout Christian, he immediately attempted to speak to the emperor and Saint Ambrose, both of whom refused to speak to him. Priscillian returned to Trier, where in 385 AD he and five of

---

191. *Theodosian Code*, 16.1.2, p. 440.
192. Homes Dudden, p. 38.

his adherents were burned alive for heresy. A grand commission to invade Spain and kill Priscillianists *en masse* was only prevented by the vigorous efforts of St. Martin, who "never afterwards could be induced to show himself in any gathering of bishops."[193]

In 388, Theodosius seized total control of the empire, and came under the influence of Saint Ambrose. The unfortunate incidents at Raqqa (formerly called Callinicum) in Syria illustrate this imperial tutelage. At Raqqa, a bishop had instigated his congregation to burn a Jewish synagogue, and, furthermore, some orthodox monks had burnt a village chapel belonging to the Valentinian Gnostics. Such acts of religious mayhem had recently become far too common in the empire, and vigorous measures were needed to stop them. Theodosius ordered the bishop to make restitution and rebuild the synagogue, but Ambrose stopped the emperor from doing so. This may seem unlikely, but Homes Dudden has the full story. The Christians got away with their vandalism, and Theodosius dropped the whole matter. This was a divisive and dangerous precedent.

In the year 390, for the first time in history, the Roman people witnessed, with horror, the public burning of male prostitutes, dragged from the homosexual brothels of Rome.[194]

Christianity was established. It was now time to tend to the pagans.

---

193. Homes Dudden, p. 233.
194. Brown, Peter: *The Body and Society*, p. 383.

The Death of Zeus

The final Christian persecution of the pagans began in the year 391 AD. It seems to have been successful, perhaps because there was no pagan tradition of glorifying religious martyrs. However, it was divisive: although the pagans may have refused martyrdom, the revolt of Arbogast and his nomination of the pseudo-Christian Eugenius as emperor caused domestic trouble for Theodosius at a time when he and the empire could least afford it. Few modern readers will give Theodosius high marks for abolishing the Olympic Games in 393 AD; this was not statesmanship but fanaticism.

Anti-pagan atrocities first broke out in Alexandria, the original home of Christianity. The temples of the gods still survived, but by law could not be used; although they were deserted monuments to past error, they were still symbols of heresy and impurity to the new and dangerous class of Christians who lived in the monasteries of the Egyptian desert. They began to form themselves into terrorist bands, armed with giant cudgels called "Israels," and systematically looted pagan homes and temples. The cry of the Tunisian Circumcellians ("Praise be to God") struck fear into the hearts of all pagans who heard it.

The destruction of the temple of Serapis at the hand of Archbishop Theophilus ("a bold, bad man, whose hands were alternately polluted with gold and with blood"[195]) may have included a much graver disaster—Gibbon charges that the destruction of the temple brought about the destruction of the "daughter library" of Alexandria.[196] The destruction of the library of Alexandria (or its dispersion) remains a vexing question for historians. The one sure fact is that the library is no longer in existence.

Theophilus was succeeded by his nephew St. Cyril, who grew jealous of the popularity of the lectures of Hypatia, the daughter of the mathematician Theon. Daily, before her academy, a long train of chariots waited while she discoursed on Plato, Aristotle, and various mathematicians. So Cyril dispatched his mob against her—a mob of many monks. Stripped naked in the street, she was dragged into a church and killed by the club of Peter the Reader. The corpse was cut to pieces, the flesh was scraped from the bones with shells, and the remnants cast into a fire. Cyril was never called to account for this frightful crime.

"So ended Greek philosophy in Alexandria."[197] From this point on, people were only allowed to think as they were ordered by the ecclesiastical authority. Justinian at last ordered the closing of all the schools of philosophy.

Cyril also expelled the Jews from Alexandria. Numbering some forty thousand and with some seven hundred years of residence in the city, they were surprised by an unprovoked raid at daybreak. The Christian soldiers were rewarded with rapine and the rich loot from Jewish homes and synagogues. The surviving Jews were then expelled—permanently.

---

195. Gibbon, chap. 28.

196. Parsons, E. A.: *The Alexandrian Library* (Amsterdam, 1952) seems to deny this charge, while others accept it.

197. Draper, John William: *History of the Conflict between Religion and Science*, pp. 54-56 (New York, 1897).

THE FALL OF ROME

In December of the year 406, a bitter winter chill enabled hordes of barbarian warriors—some 15,000—to walk with their horses, wives and children across the Rhine River. Once across the river, they plundered and destroyed at their leisure, seizing the city of Rome four years later.

The sack of Rome was a monstrous slaughter. The streets were filled with dead bodies which remained without burial. Forty thousand slaves had their bloody revenge on former masters; rape and pillage were the rule of the conquering barbarians, who freely tortured wealthy Romans in order to discover where their secret riches were hidden.

The news went out, through the empire, as a shock which spelled the end of the world as the citizens had known it. The Eternal City, which had stood for 1,163 years, was no more.

It is not often noted that both parties to this massacre were Christians. The citizens of Rome and the invading Goths under Alaric held the same faith, as is shown by the orders given to the barbarian troops not to harm the churches. A few Romans did indeed escape the bloodbath by taking shelter within the basilicas.

The pagans of that time blamed the disaster on the Christians. "See," the argument went, "we told you so. You took the statue of Victory out of the senate house and you ignored the gods of Rome, and now you see your reward. Rome is sacked!"

Gibbon agreed with this argument, by and large, and it does give the judicious mind reason to pause. Christianity had destroyed the old faith which had given stability to the Roman state. It had also declared war on the classic culture—on science, philosophy, literature and art. It had turned men's minds from the present world to a distracting and enfeebling preparation for the next world. It had led them to seek individual salvation through faith, rather than collective security through the State. It preached peace and nonviolence when the empire's survival demanded a martial spirit. Christ's victory implied Rome's death.[198]

There may be some truth in this harsh indictment. When both sides in the fight are Christian, it would seem difficult to absolve both of them.

But the counterattack was swift. Augustine opened his *City of God* with the claim that the Goths' kind treatment of the churches was a sure proof of the divine truth of Christianity, and elaborated a much larger argument from that peculiar opening.

Some decades later, the counterattack was refined, by the Church Father Salvian, who advanced the idea that Rome was destroyed by indulgence—particularly sexual indulgence. A new scapegoat was found for the fall of Rome—homosexual men.

This explanation, which is not only false but magical, is a lie which has been endlessly repeated by Christians of all stripes. For many years, it was a received dogma in some quarters that "homosexuality caused the fall of

---

198. Durant, Will: *Caesar and Christ*, p. 667.

Rome," and the nonsensical claim is still heard today—although it must be admitted that nowadays it seems to survive only in the lower social strata, where television evangelists reign.

The End

Afterword

During Late Antiquity, everyone believed in demons. Christians and pagans hardly disagreed on the subject.

Similarly, it seems there was a near-universal belief in magic. This does much to explain the multitude of laws passed against the practice of magic by the Christian emperors.

Unfortunately, science and magic were viewed as the same thing, equally evil and equally condemned. It took a long time to sort out this confusion, which only began to fade with the rise of the scientific method. It then became clear that science encompassed those things which worked and could be explained, while magic was the term for things which did not work and could not be explained.

The rise of the scientific method did not put an end to the difficulties between Christianity and science. The celebrated troubles with Galileo seem not to have taught the church anything—it repeated the same errors with Darwin. It seems easy to predict that the church is going to have enormous difficulties dealing with the new evidence for the genetic origins of male homosexuality.[199]

---

199. It is instructive to note that Buddhism, a religion constructed on the model of Aristotle rather than Plato, has never had a recorded difference of opinion with any scientific fact.

This evidence has been accumulating for some decades, beginning with pioneering twin studies in the 1930s. The twin evidence was long ignored, but now we have the brain studies of LeVay, new and exhaustive studies of twins, and new evidence from studying DNA itself: the only thing which would seem to satisfy all the evidence is a strong genetic basic to sexual orientation.

The case is by no means closed—on the contrary, the race for understanding has just begun. No matter how much one would like to embrace the genetic explanation, it is clear that there is some "Factor X" lying between the genotype and the phenotype of male homosexuality. The concordance between identical twins is not 100 percent—it's about 60 percent. In addition, there are many kinds of homosexuality, and it would not be a great surprise to find several genetic factors acting in concert—with other genes, with the hormones present during pregnancy, and with other factors in the later environment.

However faulty this brief sketch may be, it seems certain that the church will have a completely different reaction, because it has invested 1,600 years in a totally mistaken conception of male homosexuality. As Francis Bacon remarked, "radical errors in the first concoction of the mind are not to be cured by the excellence of functions and remedies subsequent." The church has long believed that homosexual men were creatures of Satan, and now it appears that "God makes homosexuals."

What are Christians to do?

The church has pilloried and denigrated gay men for well over a thousand years. Indeed, by the 1950's, the confusion was such that homosexuality was held to be simultaneously a crime, a mental illness, and a deadly sin. The hands of the church are stained with blood.

What to do?

History suggests one instructive parallel.

We have noted, several times, the parallel fates of Jews and homosexuals under the Christian hegemony. St. John Chrysostom was only the most prominent Christian voice which hated them both. For centuries, the church supported the ghettoes for European Jews, and it was even suspected of collaborating with Hitler in his Final Solution.

The result was an abrupt reversal of church policy after the Second World War, a formal apology to the Jews of the world, and a definitive order from the Vatican to stop blaming Jews for the death of Jesus. "Christ-killer" vanished from the lexicon of the church. This was a courageous step indeed for the Popes of Rome.

A similar step needs to be taken, now, with regard to gay men and women around the globe. Church policy in this area does not need modification, it needs *reversal*. A formal apology to the gay community is needed, and it is needed now. "Sodomy" must be banished from the vocabulary of Christians, and it must be banished now. Anything else is sloth, error, and grievous lack of charity, directly contradicting the teachings of Christ, who told us to love our neighbors as ourselves. Moreover, it will fix one of the worst problems of contemporary Christianity—in many quarters the religion is viewed as having just the one article of faith: "hate homosexuals." It would be fatal to link the religion with such a doctrine, and the bind needs to be severed—now.

Appendix A:

St. John Chrysostom's Defense of Monasticism

(Translated from the French, *Oeuvres Complètes de S. Jean-Chrysostome*, M. L'Abbé Joly, 8 vols., Paris/Nancy 1865. Vol. 4, pp. 217-220: the third book of Chrysostom's *Against the Opponents of the Monastic Life*.)

But I have not yet come to the most important point, the worst sort of licentiousness. Until now, modesty has restrained my tongue, but today I will overrule myself and speak. For what criminal cowardice would it not be if, seeking to extinguish this evil living, this fatal ruin, I hesitated to say a single word, as if silence alone would make it vanish! Yes, let us point out this deadly plague, even if it must cover our face with the blush of modesty. If an ulcer needs to be cleansed of putrefaction, the doctor does not hesitate to take up his sharpest knife—what am I saying?—he will plunge his very fingers into the wound! So we should not retreat from confronting this odious wound of the soul, in spite of the revolting infamy of its character.

Let us see: what is this ulcer? Has not a new and criminal love invaded the world of our own time? A licentiousness as fatal as it is incurable, the most hateful of all ruinations? A new crime, the very idea of which causes nausea and disgust? It shocks and offends not only the written laws of man, but the more sacred laws of nature. Fornication seems almost nothing when compared to this monstrosity; and, just as with sickness a new bout of pain extinguishes the feeling of a former, less acute pain, so too the enormity of this sin almost obliterates the enormity of its predecessor—a very grave sin—obscene activites with women. How happy would a man be to be able to escape the traps of this abominable passion [for women]!

Alas, we must *now* fear that women will become useless, if everywhere young men usurp their role!

But the worst of the evil is that this abominable crime shows itself in public with complete impunity. Although it is contrary to all laws, the average man might call it legitimate and lawful—for has it not passed into custom? No one blushes at all; no one dislikes it; no one shivers, revolted by horror. What am I saying? the guilty are as proud of their crimes as of their gallant speeches to the ladies. In their eyes, modest-men are madmen! Those who dare to give them sage reprimands are, according to *them*, extravagant madmen...Reproach them, if you dare: if they are stronger than you, they will beat you with no mercy; if weaker, they will content themselves with mockery, jeering, and a thousand pungent jests at your expense.

The laws have lost their authority, the magistrates their energy; preceptors, fathers, counsellors and friends go unheeded. The latter are corrupted with money, while the former think of one thing only—receiving their salaries.

Among the wise, who cherish the salvation of those in their charge, some let themselves be easily seduced and led astray, while others fear the power of these libertines. A man suspected of an attack against the freedom of his own country will more easily escape the vengeance of his fellow-citizens, than will a child escape from the infamy these perverts seek to cover him with. So it is, that in the center of our cities, men give themselves up to other men just as shamelessly as if they lived in the wildest desert.

If one is lucky enough to escape the crime itself, he will never escape the suspicion: first of all because the number of innocents is so very low—and they are lost and confounded with the multitude of criminals—*[Boswell leaves off here]* and, in the second place, because these abominable men, these demons of perversity, have only one road to revenge for the disdainful welcome given to their propositions—having failed to besmear another soul with their infamy, they make up for it by trying to spoil the other's honor and steal away his reputation. *[Festugière leaves off here]*

How many times have I not seen men wonder that a new rain of sulphur has not set our city ablaze, is not indeed setting it on fire at this very moment? Yes, they are *astounded* that the fire which devoured Sodom does not devour our own city—our city being even more worthy of punishment, since she does not use the disaster which I recall to you as a guide to correct her ways. The sight of the region, divinely incinerated, may well have been crying out for two thousand years, telling all creation to flee this most abominable of crimes, but this voice is not heard at all, and, far from interrupting the tide of immorality, men are more shameless, more daring than ever, and act only *to swell the torrent*. One would say that they were duelling with God, and even more—that they were burning to prove their lust for this crime, which God has already punished by the weight of the gravest calamities.

But why do these rains not fall to set us ablaze? How can it be that the crimes of Sodom, duplicated within our walls, do not provoke the same disasters? This comes about because God has something *in reserve* for punishment—a fire fatal in a very different way, a fire which will burn *forever* without ever consuming its prey. In the long time of the early ages, men dared graver crimes than those which provoked the Flood, and yet the earth and its people were not again drowned beneath the waters. Why this Divine Tolerance? Always the same answer—there is another fire in reserve to overwhelm the guilty.

Yes, this is the question: why, in the first ages of the world, when there were no magistrates, no written laws, no personalities regulated to follow duty, no legions of prophets to guide and direct, no threat of hellfire, no hope of heaven, no education public or otherwise, no prodigies which could have transformed and softened the nature of the very stones, yes! why were the men of those times stricken with such disastrous punishments—while men of modern times, who rejoice in the possession of all these priceless advantages, and who see and hear everywhere nothing but the scarifying language of the prophets (organs of God), of the tribunals (organs of society)—why do they not suffer the same punishments, being guilty of the same crimes? The least developed intelligence imaginable!—such a minimal intelligence can see clearly that the criminals of our own time are spared in view of a chastisement a thousand times more baleful than that which smote Sodom, or the Flood which drowned the human race! The licentiousness which we witness causes disgust and a nauseated indignation. Judge whether God, who has His eye on the universe, does not condemn the enormity of so many crimes to eternal execration, and whether He would ever let them go unpunished! Yes, be sure: God will punish these abominable and heinous crimes. On the guilty, He will press all the strength of His arm, will smite them with a wound so painful, will stir up their misery so enormously, that the fires which devoured Sodom will seem a mere bagatelle by comparison.

And in fact, such defilement goes much further than the monstrous barbarians! It even goes to a disorder unknown to the instincts of the wild animals! *[Boswell resumes here]* We find animals with a powerful sexual instinct, an instinct even as strong as madness, but they never cross the laws of nature, and even in their greatest rages, still keep within their proper limits. *[Festugière resumes here]*

But men, beings purportedly rational, illuminated by the light of a celestial learning, who teach others of morality, of the good and evil of this or that action, who hear the explanation of the Holy Scriptures, these men dare to burn more ardently for those of their own sex than for courtesans—what an odious inversion! To flaunt these revolting lusts—it is to act as if men could no longer be believed; as if there were no Providence attentive to all our needs, which judges their character and merit; it is to act as if impenetrable shadows hide us from His sight. O crown of misfortunes! Fathers of outraged boys maintain a cowardly silence, when they should be praying that the bowels of the earth might open and bury their shame along with the shame of their sons. They should be willing to sacrifice anything to do away with this licentiousness. *[Boswell stops here]*

Ah, they should send their sons far away, even over the seas, to savage islands, to the extremities of the earth [Festugière reads: "even to the heavens themselves"], they should try anything, make any sacrifice to spare them from such defilement! During a plague which menaces the life of everyone, fathers will save their children at any price, even when they have not yet fallen ill. And when the contagion which I describe to you, O fathers, has triumphed everywhere, alas! will you not only leave your sons as fodder for the vicious, but reject as "corrupters" the charitable men who would save them? Will not such perversity bring the wrath of heaven, and the most vengeful of flames?

What! for the vain pleasure of decorating their minds and memories with profane science, to hold so worthless these young souls, to let them dive into the mire of crime, and, far from being alarmed at the situation, to go so far as to *hamper* the efforts of the man virtuous enough to try for their salvation? Tell us, do you dare to claim that youth will find its salvation living in the midst of such corruption? *[Festugière stops here]*

What logic supports you? Alas, the very few who are bold enough to escape these excesses of corruption, these unlimited and universal passions, will not escape the clutches of the love of money and the spur of glory. And how many do we not see—wailing in slavery to this double chain of avarice and pride on the one hand, and the grip of the sin of Sodom on the other?

If it is a question of teaching your children worldly knowledge, you will of course avoid anything which could interfere with their studies, you will seek everything which could be of help, you will select masters, you will lavish money effortlessly, keeping all who could be obstacles at a distance; you stimulate their ardor with more zeal than Olympic trainers, telling them that ignorance leads to poverty, while knowledge is their key to fortune. There is no means we do not employ, no exhortation which we do not make ourselves (or through others) to guide them to the wished-for goal, object of all our hopes and uncertainties—and not always successful, after all this.

But when it is a question of forming a child's morals, of imprinting in his heart the principles of wisdom—still challenged by many and surrounded by so many obstacles—you persuade yourself that the thing will happen of itself! O most fatal of errors! That which is most essential, you put in last place, and that which is least essential is the object of all your desire! For virtue is as superior to knowledge as works are superior to words, and virtue is very hard to acquire: easy to talk about but difficult to do!

But is it necessary, you say to me, that my children be philosophers, that they be formed by the rules of such a religious discipline?—*There*, in that question itself, lies the source of all evil and of the general corruption: to see as bootless and useless that which is the fundamental base of our existence. See here: if your son were seriously ill, would you ask "What good is a healthy and vigorous constitution to my son?" Ah, what tears you would not shed! What efforts and precautions would you not take to restore him to health and prevent relapses! But the diseases of the soul—no one thinks of healing them. What good is all this worrying, you dare to say, and still claim the name of father! What? you reply, is everyone therefore called to this sublime philosophy, would the world go to ruin if there were no hermits?—It is not philosophy, O my friend, but the lack of philosophy which ruins the world. From *whom* come the disorders which afflict us? From those who live as devout monks, observing the laws of morality and Christian wisdom, or from people whose only conern is to serve their sensual appetites, to give themselves, daily, newer and more guilty pleasures? Who are the true philosophers, those who are content with their lot, or those who dream only of possessing that which they have not? Those who only go out accompanied by a swarm of servants and flatterers, or thos who are content with a single serving-man? (for I do not speak yet of the highest perfection, but limit myself to what is possible for anyone in the world.) To the former, honors, precedence and praise are necessary, no matter what the price! Unfortunate the man who does not advance to hail them, the man who does not salute them first, who does not lower his head and crawl in their presence! You will see them declaiming their own merit, preferring themselves to all others, believing themselves entitled to do anything and say anything. They lodge only in sumptuous buildings, sit only at the most delicately served tables, accumulate gain on gain, wealth upon wealth, landholding upon landholding. The others—humble and modest—are not afraid to have masters. They take last place without spite and strive to curb the passions which they fear as potential tyrants. They resign themselves to not owning even a fistful of land, and far from devoting themselves to usury, they possess goods only to comfort those who have them not. They keep their gaze fixed on the baseness of perishable nature—very different from those men who do not wish even to recognize it, who in their insolent pride take pains to identify themselves as *men*. *Those* will maintain courtesans, and bring defilement to the marriage bed, while the others may even abstain from the lawful contact. Yes, *those* are the men who, like furious winds, revolt against every wise discipline, avoid anyone at all who would seek their salvation, ignore those who, like guardian lanterns placed in an obscure night, show to the voyagers lost on this stormy sea, the means to regain the port and escape the tempest; and *those* are also the men who must be blamed for the wars and seditions which desolate the human race, *must* be blamed for various calamities—the burning of cities, captivity, murders, flood, plague and famine, droughts, earthquakes and other pains which heavenly justice employs to chastise the crimes of earth!

Such are the men who overturn the social order and drag it to ruin. Yes! those men call down the gravest calamities on us, men of calm and peaceful nature. There is more: these men torment the others, trouble them, and deliver them up to persecution in every sense of the word...[200]

(John Chrysostom concludes this diatribe against homosexuality and luxury—viewed as virtually synonymous, following the ideology of Philo—by asserting that the city of Antioch represents a clear and present danger to the purity of young males, a danger so great that the only possible solution is to confine *all males* to monasteries during the "dangerous years," presumably from about eight years of age to about twenty-five. The idea of *eradicating homosexuality* by confining lusty young men to same-sex prisons for ten or twenty years is a true original in the history of ideas, and has not received much support.)

---

200. Both Boswell and Festugière edit this passage to remove all reference to Sodom.

Appendix B:

Edward Gibbon's Sexual Intolerance

Edward Gibbon was a man of many masks. In particular, during the composition of his work he attempted to conceal, beneath a placid but finally devastating irony, his mounting horror of Christianity and what he felt it had done to the world.

Even if Gibbon had been personally tolerant of homosexuals, he would hardly have dared to commit *such* sentiments to print. Same-sex relations were still a serious offence; the death penalty was still in force in England.

Justinian

The reign of Justinian was marked by vigorous anti-sodomy laws, and vigorous prosecution of them. I quote most of Gibbon's discussion of these developments:

> I touch with reluctance, and dispatch with impatience, a more odious vice, of which modesty rejects the name, and nature abominates the idea. The primitive Romans were infected by the example of the Etruscans and Greeks; in the mad abuse of prosperity and power every pleasure that is innocent was deemed insipid; and the Scantinian law, which had been extorted by an act of violence, was insensibly abolished by the lapse of time and the multitude of criminals. By this law the

rape, perhaps the seduction, of an ingenuous youth was compensated as a personal injury by the poor damage of ten thousand sesterces, or fourscore pounds; the ravisher might be slain by the resistance or revenge of chastity; and I wish to believe that at Rome, as in Athens, the voluntary and effeminate deserter of his sex was degraded from the honours and the rights of a citizen. But the practice of vice was not discouraged by the severity of opinion: the indelible stain of manhood was confounded with the more venial transgressions of fornication and adultery; nor was the licentious lover exposed to the same dishonour which he impressed on the male or female partner of his guilt. From Catullus to Juvenal, the poets accuse and celebrate the degeneracy of the times; and the reformation of manners was attempted by the reason and authority of the citizens, till the most virtuous of the Caesars proscribed the sin against nature as a crime against society.

A new spirit of legislation, respectable even in its error, arose in the empire with the religion of Constantine. The laws of Moses were received as the divine original of justice, and the Christian princes adapted their penal statutes to the degrees of moral and religious turpitude. Adultery was first declared to be a capital offense: the frailty of the sexes was assimilated to poison or assassination, to sorcery or parricide; the same penalties were inflicted on the passive and active guilt of paederasty; and all criminals, of free or servile condition, were either drowned, or beheaded, or cast alive into the avenging flames. The adulterers were spared by the common sympathy of mankind, but the lovers of their own sex were pursued by general and pious indignation: the impure manners of Greece still prevailed in the cities of Asia, and every vice was fomented by the celibacy of the monks and clergy. Justinian relaxed the punishment at least of female infidelity: the guilty spouse was only condemned to solitude and penance, and at the end of two years might be recalled to the arms of a forgiving husband. But the same emperor declared himself the implacable enemy of unmanly lust, and the cruelty of his persecution can scarcely be excused by the purity of his motives. In defiance of every principle of justice, he stretched to past as well as future offences the operations of his edicts, with the previous allowance of a short respite for confession and pardon. A painful death was inflicted by the amputation of the sinful instrument, or the insertion of sharp reeds into the pores and tubes of most exquisite sensibility; and Justinian defended the propriety of the execution, since the criminals would have lost their hands had they been convicted of sacrilege. In this state of disgrace and agony two bishops, Isaiah of Rhodes and Alexander of Diospolis, were dragged through the streets of Constantinople, while their brethren were admonished by the voice of a crier to observe this awful lesson, and not to pollute the sanctity of their character. Perhaps these prelates were innocent. A sentence of death and infamy was often founded on the slight and suspicious evidence of a child or a servant: the guilt of the green faction,[201] of the rich, and of the enemies of Theodora, was presumed by the judges, and paederasty became the crime of those to whom no crime could be imputed. A French philosopher has dared to remark that whatever is secret must be doubtful, and that our natural horror of vice may be abused as an engine of tyranny. But the favourable persuasion of the same writer, that a legislator may confide in the taste and reason of mankind, is impeached by the unwelcome discovery of the antiquity and extent of the disease.[202]

---

201. The "green faction," implausibly enough, was one of two factions cheering against each other in the sporting contests of the Roman circus. They were opposed by the "red faction." Like modern soccer fans, their enthusiasm sometimes spilled into the streets. But imperial prosecution of opposing sports enthusiasts would seem to be a genuine rarity in human history.

202. Gibbon, vol. 4, chapter 44, pp. 535–537.

As usual, the footnotes yield valuable information. On the Scantinian law, Gibbon is as accurate as any modern chronicler: "The name, the date, and the provisions of this law are equally doubtful."

In support of his erroneous claim that the Athenians had a custom of degrading citizens from their office for homoerotic behavior, he cites "the oration of AEschines against the catamite Timarchus." Gibbon is quite wrong in his reading of this text; this was a common error which has only recently been cleared up by Sir Kenneth Dover, whose discoveries have been outlined above ("Greece: The Legal Situation").

On the "most virtuous of the Caesars," Gibbon notes that "Theodosius abolished the subterranean brothels of Rome, in which the prostitution of both sexes was acted with impunity."

Finally, Gibbon notes, in his footnote which tours the world: "I believe, and hope, that the negroes, in their own country, were exempt from this moral pestilence." It is strange to see Gibbon resorting to belief and hope on what is evidently a matter of simple fact, yet his statement here was to ferment, and develop, over the centuries, into what may be called the myth of black African innocence. This myth is like all others.[203]

After perusing these selections, the reader will probably agree that Gibbon hardly seems to be unbiased.

---

203. For the most comprehensive bibliography in print to date, see Dynes, Wayne and Foster, Stephen: "Homosexuality in Sub-Saharan Africa: An Unnecessary Controversy," in *Gay Books Bulletin* #9, pp. 20–21 (Gay Academic Union, New York, 1983).

BIBLIOGRAPHY

Aristophanes: *The Clouds*, trans. Arrowsmith (New York, undated).

Aristotle: *The Complete Works*, ed. Barnes (Princeton, 1984).

Boswell, John: *Christianity, Social Tolerance, and Homosexuality* (Chicago, 1980).

Brongersma, Edward: *Loving Boys* (The Netherlands and New York, 1986).

Buffière, Felix: *Üros Adolescent* (Paris, 1980).

Bullough, Vern: *Sexual Variance in Society and History* (Chicago, 1981).

Caelius Aurelianus: *On Acute Diseases* and *On Chronic Diseases*, trans. Drabkin (University of Chicago Press).

Clarke, W.M.: "Achilles and Patroclus in Love," *Hermes*, 106, pp. 381-96.

Crompton, Louis: "Gay Genocide from Leviticus to Hitler," in Crew, Louie: *The Gay Academic* (Palm Springs, 1978).

Dick, Bernard F.: *The Hellenism of Mary Renault* (Southern Illinois University Press, 1972).

Dover, K.J.: *Greek Homosexuality* (New York, 1978).

Driver, G. R. and Miles, John C.: *The Babylonian Laws* (Oxford, 1955).

Durant, Will: *Caesar and Christ* (New York, undated).

Durant, Will: *The Life of Greece* (New York, undated).

Dworkin, Andrea: *Right-Wing Women* (New York, 1983).

Dynes, Wayne R.: *Homolexis* (New York, 1985).

Dynes, Wayne R.: "Rome" (unpublished ms.)

Eusebius: *The Life of Constantine*, in *Select Library of the Nicene and Post-Nicene Fathers* (Grand Rapids, 1952).

Flacelière, Robert: *Love in Ancient Greece*, trans. Cleugh (New York, 1962).

Gibbon, Edward: *The Decline and Fall of the Roman Empire.* AMS reprint of the edition of J. B. Bury (1909-14), New York, 1974.

Grant, Michael: *The Fall of the Roman Empire* (1976).

Greenberg, David F.: *The Construction of Homosexuality* (Chicago, 1988).

Herdt, Gilbert H.: *Guardians of the Flutes* (New York, 1981).

Jaeger, Werner: *Paideia* (New York, 1979).

Horace: *The Essential Horace*, trans. Raffel (San Francisco, 1983).

Horner, Tom: *Jonathan Loved David* (Philadelphia, 1978).

Karno, Arlen: "Homosexuality in History" in Marmor, Judd: *Homosexual Behavior* (New York, 1980).

Lambert, W. G.: "Morals in Ancient Mesopotamia," Van Het Vooraziatisch-Egyptisch Genootschap, ex Oriente Lux, *Jaarbericht* No. 15 (1957-58).

Licht, Hans (pseud. Paul Brandt): *Sexual Life in Ancient Greece* (New York, 1974).

MacMullen, Ramsay: "Roman Attitudes to Greek Love," *Historia*, 31, 1982, pp. 484-502.

Marrou, H.I.: *A History of Education in Antiquity* (New York, 1964).

Oaks, Robert F.: "Defining Sodomy in Seventeenth-Century Massachusetts," *Journal of Homosexuality*, vol. 6, nos. 1/2, Fall/Winter 1980/81.

Plato, *The Collected Dialogues*, ed. Hamilton and Cairns (Princeton, 1971).

Rudd, Niall: *The Satires of Horace and Persius* (Penguin, 1973).

Schweitzer, Albert: *The Quest of the Historical Jesus* (New York, 1961.)

Sergent, Bernard: *Homosexuality in Greek Myth* (Boston, 1986).

Syme, Ronald: *Ammianus and the Historia Augusta* (Oxford, 1968).

Theocritus: *Idylls and Epigrams*, trans. Hine (New York, 1982).

Theognis: *Elegies*, in *Hesiod and Thegnis*, trans. Wender (Penguin, 1976).

Vanggaard, Thorkild: *Phallos* (New York, 1982).

Weinrich, James D.: *Sexual Landscapes* (New York, 1987).

Westermarck, Edward: *The History of Human Marriage* (New York, 1922).

INDEX

A

Achilles the, 21, 40-42, 44, 49, 185
Æschines, 42
Antinous, 66-67
Aristophanes, 26, 40, 50-51, 185
   The Clouds, 26, 50-52, 113, 185
Aristotle, 7, 33-35, 37-39, 41, 65, 90, 105, 112, 130, 146, 164, 169, 185
   Nichomachean Ethics, 35, 37
   Politics, 15-16, 34-35, 56, 86
Artz, 27, 29
Aurelius Victor, 64

B

barbarism, 11-12
Boswell, 10, 62-63, 70-72, 76, 112, 124, 129, 153, 155, 175-177, 180, 185

C

Cælius Aurelianus, 38
Council of Jerusalem, 70, 72

cruelty, 55-56, 61, 183
Cyrnus, 44-47, 53

D

David and Jonathan, 73
Diocletian, 55-56, 145, 147, 149
Dodds, 31
Durant, 16, 166, 185-186
Dworkin, 70-71, 186

E

Elagabalus, 59, 64
Erasmus, 26
Eros, 20, 26, 47, 57, 96, 104

F

Flacelière, 53-54, 186

G

Gibbon, 8-10, 12, 16, 28, 53, 62, 80, 102, 146-147, 152, 160, 164, 166, 181, 183-184, 186
Greek education, 18

H

Hadrian, 58, 66-67
Harmodios and Aristogeiton, 21
Hebrews, 19, 88
    Babylonian exile, 76, 88-89, 119
Hellenism, 8, 17, 20, 92, 94, 185
Homer, 17, 21, 40-44, 49
    Odyssey, 42-43
Horace, 59-61, 186-187

I

Islam, 11, 144

J

Jæger, 40, 44, 47

L

lesbians, 70
Leviticus, 68-76, 88-89, 124, 127-128, 142, 185
Lex Julia de adulteriis, 62-63
Lex Scantinia, 62-63
Licht, 44, 54, 134, 186

M

Maccabees, 17, 93-94
Marrou, 16, 18, 41, 187

N

Nero, 59

O

Ovid, 59

P

Paganism, 9, 11, 27, 72, 75, 158
Papua New Guinea, 48
pederasty, 7, 12, 15-22, 29, 33, 37-41, 44, 48-49, 51, 53, 57, 59, 61, 82, 89, 95, 105, 110, 136, 138, 140
Persia, 36
Philip the Arab, 64
    Charmides, 22-24
    Phaedrus, 138

R

Republic, 24, 28, 34, 55-56, 58-60, 63

S

Speech of Diotima, 29
Symposium, 22, 29, 41-42, 47, 105
The Last of the Wine, 20

Rome, 7-8, 55-58, 60, 62-63, 65-66, 127, 144-145, 148-149, 153, 155, 161-162, 165-167, 171, 182, 184, 186
Scriptores historiæ Augustæ, 64
Severus Alexander, 64
Sextus Empiricus, 65
slavery, 58, 177
Socrates, 7, 20, 22-24, 26-31, 34, 41-42, 50, 52
sodomy, 13, 71, 76, 110, 139, 171, 187
Solon, 53
Soranus, 38

T

temple prostitution, 73, 79
Ten Commandments, 71-73, 133-134, 140, 144
Theognis, 40, 44-48, 50-51, 53, 187
Trinity, 28, 102

V

Vanggaard, 19, 36, 40, 48, 187
Virgil, 59

X

Xenophon, 20, 41, 104

CPSIA information can be obtained
at www.ICGtesting.com
Printed in the USA
BVHW041742110922
646766BV00013B/73